adventures of your own and reminisce about journeys past. A must-read for anyone with a passion for exploration and discovery." —MJ Jamieson

"Nearly everyone has a travel story, but not everyone can make you feel as if you're on a journey alongside them. *Soul-Stirring Essays About the Travel That Changed Us* does just that. It goes beyond describing destinations to bring you into the depths of the authors' personal transformations. Whether you love to travel or simply appreciate compelling, heartfelt stories, this book is sure to entertain and inspire."
—Rose Hartwig

"*Going Places* is a treasure trove of travel story gems. The personal accounts shared in this book are intimate, rich and inspiring. If you enjoy exploring deep and honest human experiences through the lens of travel, this book is for you!"
— Carrie Contey, PhD, Clarity Coach

Paperback: 979-8-9880332-5-7

Ebook: 979-8-9880332-4-0

Edited by Erin Althaus, Kristi Koeter, and Michelle Savage

Cover art by Christy Jaynes

Sulit Press

www.sulitpress.com

GOING PLACES

Soul-Stirring Essays About The Travel That Changed Us

Amanda Nitschke

Jason Fuerstenberg

Michelle Savage

Vincent McNeeley

Julie Candelon

Natasha Zike

Debra Blue

Janene Niblock

Oswald Perez

Diana Maldonado

Susie Moceri

Kalpashree Gupta

SULIT PRESS

Praise for *Going Places: Soul-Stirring Essays About The Travel That Changed Us*

"*Going Places* encourages us all to think differently about what it means to travel. These authors have courageously confronted social norms and pushed past personal and physical limitations to soul-search their way across the globe." —Deepa Purushothaman, Author of *The First, The Few, The Only: How Women of Color Redefine Power in Corporate America* and Executive Fellow of Harvard Business School

"A great collection. The stories are personal and take you on an evocative journey with the author to experience travel, emotions and life learnings. A must-add to the collection for those of us who know the deep impact travel leaves on our heart and mind." —Ahana Mullick

"This book gives the reader a glimpse into the joy, pain, awe, and soul shifting nature of travel of the various authors. It's an inspiring collection of essays." —Karen Mildenhall

"Captivating and wanderlust-inducing, *Going Places* immerses readers in a world of vivid destinations and heartfelt experiences. The authors' storytelling and keen observations make each journey come alive, inviting you to embark on

Contents

Ready to fast-track your publishing career, increase your visibility, or boost your business?

H arness the power of partnership by contributing a 3,000-word chapter to one of our upcoming Multi-Author Books!

If you are...

- Inspired by what you do and want to generously share what you've learned...

- Committed to meeting deadlines and doing your best work...

- Ready to connect with other aspiring authors who are as excited as you are to share your book with the world...

Then our Multi-Author Book might be the right path for you!

Learn more at sulitpress.com/multi-author-books

Introduction

Simply put, travel is the intentional practice of moving our bodies across the earth, putting both distance and time between what we know for sure and a new experience that awaits. But it's not just a singular outcome we expect from our travels abroad. Like an acid trip that's all trip and no acid, traveling cracks open our minds to new perspectives, new ways of being, and parts of ourselves that have previously slept dormant.

Such gifts are born from a life untethered, and we don't always have to venture far or to exotic locations to receive them.

Whether we're running away from the monotony of the daily grind or flinging ourselves toward the unknown in search of an awakening, a wild adventure, or a deeper understanding of our world and the people in it, few experiences provide more bang for the buck than a plane ticket or a bus pass to somewhere else—even if it's just for a few days.

So, if traveling provides such potent transformational experiences, why do travel essays still impact readers so intensely? How can second-hand experiences espouse so much first-hand wisdom and inspiration?

Perhaps it has to do with our deep curiosity to connect with humans who speak different languages, eat different foods, and organize their communities in ways we cannot fathom. Or maybe we simply enjoy some tantalizing, budget-friendly entertainment without the threat of long layovers or malaria.

One thing that's certain about any expedition is that, even if you only travel vicariously through someone else's story, no one returns unchanged. The following essays are as much about the journeys as they are about the transformations that happened along the way. By reading this book, you may experience a spark of wanderlust, a desire to redesign your entire life, or discover a deep appreciation for everything you already have.

Michelle Savage

Founder, Sulit Press

www.sulitpress.com

1

Souvenirs for the Soul

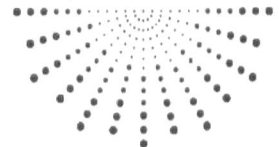

AMANDA NITSCHKE

The directions simply read, "Go to kilometer fifty. Enter the gate and walk for about twenty-five minutes through the jungle." It sounded vague. I had called for clarification to make sure nothing was lost in translation, but was told the exact same thing in both English and Spanish. So, there in Iquitos, Peru, in the heart of the Amazon jungle, I hopped into a taxi with my partner at the time. The scenery changed quickly. The bustling city was gone, replaced by a straight, two-lane road enveloped by thick trees on each side. After a friendly chat with the driver, the taxi slowed to a stop. We waved as he drove off, leaving us on the side of the road with no one and nothing in sight except for the gate in front of us.

I could barely open the gate, but I squeezed through. We started down a faint trail and stepped into another world. Dense growth towered above. The earth was slick with mud from the morning rain. Light streamed down from the green canopy of leaves and vines that dangled down to the snaking roots on the forest floor. Luminous streams meandered around the path.

I was a guest in a stranger's home, treading cautiously through the quiet, trying not to think about the well-camouflaged creatures likely lurking nearby, particularly the ones without legs! Apprehension started bubbling up, but after about thirty minutes, just as we were told, we crossed a tiny bridge that opened into a clearing with a little house on the right. Glowing in sweat and filled with relief, I knew we were in the right place. I was there to embark on my first plant medicine journey. While this was way out of my comfort zone, it was a natural extension of the healing and self-exploration I'd experienced through my yoga practice. Travel has always been a way for me to learn and grow, but nothing could have prepared me for this soul-changing adventure!

Doña Otilia, a local healer, greeted us warmly with her kind eyes and bright smile, her face round like the full moon, as she prepared for our ceremony. She was dressed simply, as anyone would be while doing chores outside in the middle of the steaming jungle. After we found our accommodation—a simple, thatched hut perched on stilts with cut-out windows along with a lovely deck and hammock looking out into the green expanse—we had time to eat, bathe, and rest before our gathering that evening. There was no syllabus or itinerary and little explanation of what to expect.

Most of the afternoon was spent relaxing and journaling as I waited for the ceremony.

I ebbed my hunger with a bit of fruit since a *dieta*, or specific diet for the plant medicine, was part of the preparation. From the hammock, I watched the bees and butterflies dance to a symphony of squawking birds and howling monkeys. Puffy white clouds morphed into creatures as they ventured through the perfectly blue sky.

Later, a young man led me to the cleansing bath in preparation for the ceremony. It was situated away from the buildings and had an itsy-bitsy teeny-weeny makeshift shower curtain. Chickens pecked around. I didn't even have a towel or change of clothes. Tentatively, I stripped off my clothing, hoping there wasn't a hungry jaguar watching me. Standing there naked and exposed, with the eyes of the vibrant jungle observing me, I quickly slipped into the cool water scattered with tiny, fragrant pink flowers. I cupped my hands and poured the water on my body. It was refreshing in the sweltering heat, but it was hard to relax. As I took a deep breath and sank into the soft support of the water, I became fully aware of the vastness that surrounded me. The container of my everyday life broke open.

At sunset, the ancient ritual with the grandmother plant, Ayahuasca, commenced. Ayahuasca is a psychoactive tea made of multiple plants that have been boiled together. It has been used by indigenous people in South America for thousands of years for healing, well-being, teaching, and spiritual guidance. While plant medicine is used for a number of maladies, including depression and addiction, I was interested in growth and expansion, open to any and all healing and teaching the medicine offered.

A mix of international visitors and locals gathered on benches on the dirt floor under a thatch covering. Doña Otilia now wore a traditional white dress decorated with brightly colored ribbons trimming her V-neck. She was assisted by another local healer, Don Hector. She came around, blowing pungent sacred tobacco smoke onto my crown and heart to cleanse my energy field. Then, one by one, we blew our intentions into the sacred brew known as the "spirit of nature."

My intention was this yoga mantra:

> *Om Namah Shivaya Gurave*
> *Saccidananda Murtaye*
> *Nisprapancaya Shantaya*
> *Niralambaya Tejase*
> *Om*

Translation:

> *I open my heart to the power of Grace*
> *That lives in us as goodness*
> *That is never absent and radiates peace*
> *And lights the way to transformation*

I choked down the thick, acrid liquid, trying not to gag, tasting the earthiness, hints of chicory, burnt coffee, and tobacco, as it coated my tongue. The taste was incomparable to anything I've ever put in my mouth. Soon after, the healers began walking around, shaking the rattles, and singing the magical *Icaros,* the medicine songs that bring the Ayahuasca to life so it can guide the journey and bestow protection, knowledge, and healing.

I waited expectantly for it to kick in. Otilia inquired periodically to see if anyone was experiencing *visiones*. My answer was still a no. Deflated,

I felt like maybe nothing was going to happen. Oh well! So much for a transcendental experience!

But suddenly, a novel sensation crept into my body and my brain. In my mind's eye, a little guy was cranking gears, slowly opening a door to the right side of my brain. I was astonished by what I was sensing in my body. Then, the scene quickly changed. The consciousness and interconnection among the trees and plants in the jungle became fully evident. The energy field of the trees emanated with rainbow auras shining above the forest. Then, a tree being that presented itself as a grandfather tree, representing all of nature, stepped forward to communicate with me, showing me images of the destruction of the earth throughout history. The grief and sorrow of what the trees have experienced as witnesses and recordkeepers of the earth's events over eons was palpable. I couldn't stop the tears from flowing. I apologized to him on behalf of humanity, making a commitment to pass on their message and contribute to the healing of the earth.

Then suddenly, my body floated up into the inky darkness, and an object emerged in the distance with a cord hanging down. Curiously, I examined it as it drifted closer and closer, and then I was stunned when it hooked up to my navel. A golden light flowed through it, and a delicious warmth poured into me, filling me with the most loving, supportive, and blissful energy. I let out a sigh in amazement. The womb of the cosmos cradled me in weightlessness, my umbilical cord connected to source, the ultimate mother. It was like an aerial refueling for airplanes, but it was replenishing my life force! The glow in my center continued to expand until I was full, and then I watched reluctantly as it detached and sailed away.

The *visiones* were certainly happening now! I connected with Doña Otilia, communicating telepathically, "Oh my god, did you see that? Did you see what just happened?" She smiled and nodded her head. She never asked me again if I was having any *visiones*. She already knew. And I knew she knew! Nonetheless, throughout all of this, I felt completely grounded in the present moment. It was like augmented reality, an overlay on everyday perception that was heightened or as if I were dreaming in the mind's eye. And it wasn't random. It had its own awareness. The medicine worked with me and the *Icaros*. My mind was absolutely blown! The ceremony came to a close, and as I went back up to the room, a wave of nausea hit me. Luckily, I made it in time to vomit out of the screenless window; this was just a part of the *limpia,* or energetic cleanse, I received from the plant medicine. What an experience I had just been through. I went to bed to sleep peacefully for the remainder of the night.

The next day, I bounced out of the jungle, feeling light and energized. Later, in the Andes mountains, as I explored the ancient Incan ruins of Ollytaytambo and Machu Picchu and scaled the mystical Huayna Picchu perched high above the ancient citadel, I had a deeper appreciation for this beautiful land with my newfound awareness.

This sentiment only grew throughout the retreat in Pisac, where I worked with the sacred cactus, Huachuma, another plant medicine, as well as Ayahuasca again. During the Huachuma ceremonies in this sacred land, I met Pachamama, the Earth Mother and creative consciousness. She came alive all around me. I saw her face in the slow-moving stones, in the trunks of trees with their waving branches, and in the towering mountains with beards of hanging growth. I felt her kisses as tiny raindrops fell on my cheeks. I heard her words on the wind, "Pachamama is *all* of creation, including you!" Before this encounter, I sometimes felt homesick, even in my everyday life. I can't even explain what I was homesick for. But after this experience, in the deepest part of my soul, I felt like I was truly home and have never felt homesick since!

During another ceremony, a flood of light beings entered through the glass roof of the hexagonal ceremonial building after assuring me that they were there to help, and I gave them permission. They joked with me about being in a trauma ward, but this was soul surgery, working on our energy bodies. I already possessed a strong awareness of my subtle body from my yoga practice (think chakra system), so that aspect wasn't new. What was, um, strange, to say the least, was having other beings work on my energy body while I was fully aware of it. Even after doing physical therapy for years, I had a residual hip injury that was healed that night. Since then, I have never had any issues with it. It's better now at forty-eight than it was when I did the Inca trail at twenty-eight on my first visit to Peru!

On the last day of the retreat, we realized the retreat ended a little later than we thought. My partner wanted to leave early; however, I wanted to stay to get closure with the group and the process as we had woven deep connections to each other throughout the experience. The hotel in Cuzco was just a short taxi ride away, so I told him that he could go and I'd meet him there in a few hours. He was not happy with that. He was confrontational and loud, looming above me. I was shocked that this conflict was even happening. I stood firm and told him that I was staying. This was all being witnessed by the group and the guide. He left, and I'd be there to join him a few hours later; no biggy, right?

After he departed, our guide, Javier, put his hands on my shoulders firmly, looked deep into my eyes, and stated, "You are so strong." While it was powerful at that moment, I somewhat shrugged it off. I didn't think I was doing anything unexpected or special, just simply standing up for myself.

Little did I know I would come to replay his words many times in the future, as that interaction was a preview of what was to come and the strength I would need to tap into.

I was so happy I stayed with the group to bring the powerful journey to completion. When I arrived back at the hotel a few hours later, my partner was nowhere to be found. I figured he ran out to get something and didn't think anything of it, and I started unpacking. However, when he returned, he was furious with me. And explosive. We argued. He said he was going to leave me in Peru. Things eventually calmed down and returned to "normal" as if there hadn't been a giant explosion. Although I was overwhelmed and distraught by his reactions, I was relieved that we had some resolve and also that I didn't have to figure out a whole new way to get home on my own. We headed back to Texas a few days later.

Despite the drama that I faced with my partner during the trip, my heart was truly overflowing with precious soul souvenirs that I had received from these sacred plant medicines. I knew I was on this planet for a reason. I understood that I was a bridge for the children that I worked with as a speech-language pathologist, helping them connect and develop speech and language. Furthermore, I realized that this medicine was, in fact, a whole other level of communication, integrating mind, body, and spirit to address "communication disorders of the soul." While I had *believed* in the oneness of creation prior to coming on the retreat, this deep awareness now permeated every single cell of my body. I knew I was connected to something bigger than myself. I discovered that there is so much beyond ourselves and our thinking in modern-day western society that every in-dividual has access to in order to facilitate our own growth, healing, and well-being. I knew this knowledge was meant to be shared. Little did I know it would set in motion a whole new journey for my future!

Several months after returning from Peru, my relationship with my partner continued its downward spiral. I ultimately realized there was no future with this relationship as it was in its current state. And then, out of nowhere, I discovered I was pregnant, very unexpectedly! I had thought it was all the spinning rides at the rodeo that had made me nauseous. A couple of months earlier, my partner had told me he didn't think he could even have kids. All it took was a one-time miscommunication (only fitting) while I was switching birth control pills. When he got back into town, I shared the news. Let's just say he wasn't exactly thrilled with this unforeseen detour.

Not sure if he was ready to be a parent, he wanted to explore all of the options. I honored his feelings and perspective and went to a consult, scheduling the potential procedure as far out as I could because I really had no intention of going through with it. I thought it was ridiculous that I was even considering this for myself at this point in my life. I had always wanted children, but it just hadn't happened yet, and I was almost thirty-seven with a solid career and a supportive family.

On the day the procedure was scheduled, I knew in my heart I couldn't go through with it. I then received a message that my nephew had just been born, which validated my choice. I knew that every time I saw him, I'd be reminded of whatever choice I made on this day. Honoring my soul, I wrote a letter to my son's father to inform him that I was having this baby whether he participated or not. (For some reason, he wasn't there that morning.) I knew I was choosing to essentially do this alone. I realized that my energetic reboot from the Ayahuasca had been not only a healing but also a soul gift for the future, preparing me to embark on this journey of pregnancy and motherhood. Perhaps the universe knew more than I did about what was to come.

We decided to try to make a go of the relationship, and he became excited about the pending arrival. After an easy pregnancy and a long labor at a birthing center, my sweet son was born via emergency C-section. When I arrived at the hospital, I was greeted by Nurse Grace and Dr. Love (I seriously can't make this stuff up!). We were in good hands! He arrived soon after, healthy and looking seriously relieved that he was finally in this world.

Not surprisingly, the relationship challenges that existed before my son was born did not improve but, in fact, worsened. While he was there for our child physically, somewhat, I was supporting all of us. I had been taking care of every single living and medical expense as well as many other responsibilities. Communication attempts and moments when I asserted myself or attempted to set boundaries resulted in him screaming and yelling, flipping couches, and throwing a glass in the sink, causing it to shatter. The insults and gaslighting escalated. I was constantly walking on eggshells. My soul was shrinking, and my sense of self was fading away. The overall unpredictability of this volatile environment was not something that could continue. I knew I needed to make a change.

We separated before my son's first birthday, and our relationship was still extremely challenging. He would threaten me or flake out on his time with our son without giving any notice, so I was left without childcare and couldn't see clients. When he was served due to lack of response, he entered my home and threw my groceries on the floor, causing a box of tomato soup to open and splatter on my favorite books on the bookshelf, and then he threw my cell phone over the fence. It was a long and expensive process to get an agreement in place because we had not been married, and he saw no reason for us to have a custody agreement in any shape or form.

During this time of conflict, I often recalled the words of Javier, our guide from Peru, which had been imprinted on my soul: You are so strong. I realized this was yet another gift that was intended for the future, helping me when I had to dig deep to find my strength. I replayed his words over and over again. I can still see his eyes staring into mine and feel the weight of his hands on my shoulders.

With all of this going on, there was no way I could physically be in all the places I needed to be or sustain the energy I needed to be fully present and engaged for my son and the exceptional kids I worked with. And there was no way I could financially keep things going as they were on my own. And dating??? Whatever! All I wanted was a nap! I was exhausted and stressed...wondering how many plates I could keep spinning until they would all come crashing down. I did not want my life to be driven by fear. I did not want to make choices because that's the way it was "supposed to be." My heart and my soul, and that of my child, were way more important than any of that! I wasn't going to let my soul get crushed.

I knew I needed help. I was using all of the tools I had as a yoga teacher and speech-language pathologist. They helped a lot, but it was clear that I had to dig deeper. Synchronistically, I found a teacher and healer who had just moved to Austin, which was ideal as I wasn't going to be taking off for the jungle of Peru any time soon to dive into my own healing. I knew I had no other option if I wanted to truly unbind myself from this situation. I had to follow this path. It wasn't even a matter of whether I wanted to or not; it was clearly a matter of soul survival.

I leapt back onto the beautiful shamanic path from the Andes with the new teacher I had found. I was initiated into this sacred lineage from Peru and received ancient rites, healings, and teachings connecting me to this indigenous tradition and, ultimately, unraveling all that I knew. To be clear, these practices and healings did not involve plant medicine this time. My soul-stirring journey two years earlier had just been the beginning. It had cracked open these seeds inside of me, sowing them deep in the soil, now ready to take root and grow. I had no idea of the latent power that those soul souvenirs possessed and how they would support me through painful and difficult times. They continued to bestow gifts as I nurtured them and allowed them to flourish through this work.

Every full moon and new moon, after my son would fall asleep, I'd go out alone in the darkness to build a fire in my backyard, communing with Pachamama, the elements, my animal allies, and my guides, learning how to engage with the earth to transmute pain and heartache, allowing the earth to receive it and becoming a co-creator in my life, working to create *ayni* or sacred reciprocity. Pachamama held me in her arms, taking my grief and anger so I could move beyond the heartache to fearlessly follow my inner compass with clarity. I knew I wasn't alone. I continued to excavate the wounds, releasing ancient stories, healing ancestral lines, and cutting cords that held me back, strengthening my relationships with myself and nature, exploring the shadow world to recapture energy and the parts of myself that had been lost.

It was the beginning of an entirely new journey of healing and growth that allowed me to tap into a strength beyond myself to navigate very challenging times and weave it into my everyday life. I was stronger and could see and feel the changes both internally as well as externally. In regards to interactions with my son's father, it was now like watching a tornado swirl from afar versus being sucked up and thrown around inside of it.

As I made these massive energetic shifts, however, there were very few people who could truly understand my perspective on life or dating or relate to my situation, even my dearest friends and family, who were amazingly supportive and helpful by caring for my son. My mom thought I was absolutely crazy for quitting my "stable" job to work for myself, but working in the school system was like trying to play a PS5 game on an Atari system. I was spending a ton of time commuting and working just to pay for the daycare I needed for that job. My friends without kids were often out having fun, while my friends with kids were up to their elbows in childrearing and trying to salvage their own marriages. At times I felt very alone, but I leaned on this energetic support team and the practices that tied me to all of the beautiful creations around me that carried me through, always showing me grace and beauty.

My healing journey and shamanic studies informed my practice as a therapist, as I could no longer ignore the "the soul piece." I also realized the significance of sharing this sacred knowledge as a spiritual guide. I began holding space for others, guiding groups of women and children through ceremony and facilitating healing sessions with this energy medicine (without plants). I truly see this path as an expansion and integration of my practice of over two decades as a pediatric speech-language pathologist and a yogi. It's all about connection and communication, mind, body, spirit, Earth...and beyond!

Ultimately, I had to awaken to a whole new way of being, shifting how I engaged in every aspect of life. I listened even more deeply to my body, to my soul, to the universe, and to my child to stay true to myself as I navigated life. This work allowed me to stay grounded, be present, and honor my intuition. I broke free of worry and the judgment of others (and myself) so I could make the best decisions for myself and my son, which was often exactly the opposite of what others thought was the logical thing I should do! I continued to hold the highest vision for my life, and I still do. People have often commented to me about how great it is that my ex and I come across as a united front in support of our son at school and soccer. But just because we are united now doesn't mean it was easy. There were countless tears and struggles...and miracles! I had to tap into something beyond myself, and it has made all the difference for myself, and my child.

Do we all need to run to Peru and take plant medicine? No! While plant medicine is beautiful and powerful, it is but one piece of an ancient spiritual path. There are many ways to expand our awareness and heal *without* it. The true medicine is in deepening connection with the self, others, and all of creation so we can peel back the layers to reveal the truest version of ourselves, bringing our divine spark into everyday life and helping it burn brightly. I tap into this medicine every day! The experiences I've had in my own healing and in the work I do with clients are equally as powerful and sometimes even more so as there is no plant medicine involved.

What began as a curiosity to explore the world through travel, along with a willingness to be open to the universe, culminated in a mind-blowing journey back to myself. It was a powerful healing experience in and of itself, but I had no idea how it would continue to impact me for years to come. The soul souvenirs that I carried home from the jungles and mountains of Peru were truly gifts for the future, more significant than I could have ever imagined, more powerful than any souvenir sitting on a shelf. Once home, they awakened and flourished to carry me through some really painful and difficult times. Today, their magic continues to unfold, not just for me and my son but for others as I guide them on their own transformational healing journeys. I cannot wait to see the gifts and growth that manifest as this sacred path, which has been so generously shared by the Qero people of Peru, is cultivated in the modern world with the intention of creating harmony and healing for our beautiful planet and all of its inhabitants.

AMANDA NITSCHKE

A manda is a spiritual mentor, speech-language pathologist, thought leader, author, and public speaker. She weaves together her yogic and shamanic practices with over twenty years of experience supporting children with neurodevelopmental disorders.

Her innovative approach stresses connection and communication on the physical, mental, and spiritual (energetic) levels. Amanda is passionate about holding space for women as they awaken to their inner power.

Amanda is inspired daily by her ten-year-old son, who is also her favorite travel buddy, and their three kitties. (No, she's not a crazy cat lady!) She's a yoga lover and a Mesa Carrier in the Q'ero tradition. She loves last-minute trips, exploring nature, and watching the magic of life unfold with her son.

Website: pachayoga.kartra.com/page/LINKS

LinkedIn: www.linkedin.com/in/amanda-nitschke/

2

Rip Currents

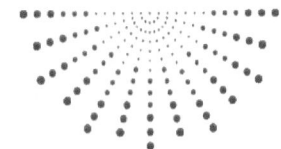

JASON FUERSTENBERG

Have you ever been caught in a rip current? I haven't, but you know those signs at the beach we all see, but ignore, that tell us how to escape being dragged aimlessly out to sea? The ones we pull our coolers and umbrellas right past, trying to find that perfect spot to stake our claim in the sand and enjoy the day? I found my life caught in a rip current that snuck up on me like a phantom wave. In a very short period of time, my life was completely falling apart. Or quite possibly, it was falling apart for a long time, but I had become so good at acting like I had my life together even to fool myself.

My marriage was ending. My wife had moved to an apartment of her own with my daughter, and I could not possibly have afforded two apartments in California. I was living in a garage because my car was repossessed, and the eviction notice to my apartment was still hanging on my apartment door as a constant reminder that I was a failure. My mental health was rapidly deteriorating. I was a small business owner, providing technical support and consulting to coffee companies, but I was finding it hard to find the motivation to work hard at my business when it was hard enough just to catch my breath. That phantom wave was dragging me hopelessly under, and I didn't know how to escape it, or if I even wanted to break free, for that matter. I needed something to happen, and at that point, I didn't care if it was good or bad, just something. What does that rip current sign say, anyway?

At a certain point, self-realization kicks in, and it becomes obvious you're fighting against the current and working very hard to go nowhere. I so badly wanted to fix everything that was not working in my life, and building a new one did not seem like an option. The idea of swimming directly back to the safe, comfortable shore wasn't even a thought in my mind. I was already so worn down, but the exhaustion of going nowhere fast and fighting the current was so overwhelming.

My work opportunities at the time had forced me to stay in the same area, always on call and ready to help someone. I was yearning so hard for a fresh start and to escape the troubles of life had me feeling desperate. I had not really traveled before, aside from family vacations growing up. Nothing against the loaded-down, wood-paneled station wagon from my youth (complete with a full-size red canoe on top) or even the annual visits to Florida to see the grandparents. Although memorable, none of those trips really defined or changed me as a person. I knew I needed to get away, and not just from the rip current of my life. Despite wanting to escape everything so badly, there were a lot of things about myself that I knew I needed to confront head-on.

Don't Swim Against The Current

Hopeless desperation really doesn't change you. My headphones were always on, blasting whatever self-development book was recommended to me by friends. I was hitting the gym and doing everything all the experts suggested would make me into the "best version of myself." Then, the terrifying reality hit. I don't even like myself, I don't trust myself, I would not even want to be my friend. And if I feel that way, why would anyone else want to be my friend? I was working so hard and could not even gain my own respect and admiration. I would ask myself questions like, "What would make me happy?" and "Who am I?" The saddest part was I didn't have the answers.

One day, I stumbled on a guided meditation. I rolled my eyes, but that desperate feeling was strong enough to fully commit. I thought, *okay, I am going to give this my all.* I am going to direct my life instead of going with the flow. I grabbed my headphones and sat down in the corner of the room. It was so dark from the blackout curtains that I couldn't see a thing without turning on my phone. I sat up straight but comfortable as the instructions informed me and poured my heart out. I was determined I would not get up until I was a different person and ready to live free of the rip currents of my life. I let go of the past, forgave myself for my failures, and leaned hard into gratitude for the opportunities of my future. I don't know how much time passed. I don't know if I felt any better, but I felt different. That hopeless desperation was gone, and I felt that this moment of transition in my life was now in my control, despite having no idea what my future held.

The very next day, I woke up and checked my emails as I normally do. One email caught my eye. It was from one of my clients, and the heading of the email read "Special Project Request, Travel Required!" My largest client could find no one to travel the country, and they were asking me to travel coast to coast! At first, I thought this might be a dream. I would need to visit coffee shops across the country to survey the stores to ensure a fancy new espresso machine was compatible. The timing was too weird to not get a coffee and wake up before replying. The opportunity to travel while still working in my field was something I had wanted so badly but had no idea how to get. By the next week, I was already starting in San Diego and working my way up the coast to Seattle and then cross-country to Florida. I was in shock—in a good way. One week ago, I was heartbroken, hopeless, and living in a garage, and now I was on an all-expenses-paid, cross-country journey. It felt amazing to escape the chaos of my life.

If You Need Help, Yell Or Wave For Assistance

One of the main reasons I was offered this opportunity was that no one else wanted to do it. It was April 2020. The pandemic had just started, and all of a sudden, I was considered an "essential worker" being asked to travel the country. Normally, the idea of traveling sparks images of exploring fun restaurants and unique places, meeting up with friends or family, or getting to know new people—none of this was even an option. Most businesses were closed. The idea of even booking a hotel was difficult because every city, county, and state had different regulations as to who was allowed to be there. Everyone I knew was staying at home and enjoying a small circle of people to quarantine with while I was getting to leave the house and experience new places. I thought I had beat the system!

Making my way up the coast was breathtakingly beautiful. I had wrapped up my work in California and was driving up the Pacific Coast Highway, with a pit stop at Redwoods National Park planned the next day on the way to Oregon. The night was getting late, and I needed to find a spot to sleep, so I booked a hotel on my phone and pulled into the small military town of Fort Bragg. I grabbed my bag and, half asleep, wandered into the hotel to check in.

"Checking in?" the guy at the motel asked.

"Yes, I have a reservation." I handed him my ID.

"Are you working in town?"

"Yes sir, I just finished and am on my way north."

"I need proof that you have a job in town, or unfortunately, you won't be allowed to stay here," he said.

"I did have a job. I finished it before checking in," I explained, showing him my work order.

"Unfortunately, if you don't have work here tomorrow, it would be against the law for you to stay here." I was sent away. Mendocino County did not want me to stay the night, apparently, so I had to sleep in my car tucked off of the highway instead.

I was completely alone and isolated. The excitement of traveling was quickly wearing off. That rip current sign was in my head again. It said, "If you need help, yell or wave for assistance." Only spending time with myself was going to be the greatest challenge I had ever faced. Most people have family and friends surrounding them in these moments of life transition. Everyone I knew was miles and miles away, self-isolating with their loved ones.

Making my way north through Portland and Seattle, I discovered that artists in nearly every city put murals up on the plywood that businesses used to board up their buildings. Everywhere I went, there were more plywood murals, and I started taking photos of them in every city. It gave me something to take my mind off of having to be my own best friend and attempting to enjoy my own company.

The pandemic made so many great cities look like empty, post-apocalyptic shells of themselves. They were depressed, empty, and dangerous. They looked like how I felt inside. As society was going through a difficult transition, so was I. But these murals were something else, a sign of hope. I began to see them as a sign that even in moments of transition, we can still make the best of things and create something beautiful. My creativity had long been in hibernation. I had bought a camera a few years prior in an attempt to share a hobby with my wife, who was always setting up elaborate photoshoots. I didn't even really know how to use my camera, but I began experimenting, walking around these abandoned cities and capturing this historical moment in time. I couldn't help but wonder if these cities would ever return to their former glory. *Would they be better than they were before? Was there a chance that everything, including my life, would be better in the future?*

If You Can't Escape, Float or Tread Water

It was my first time visiting Austin, Texas, and I couldn't have been more excited to experience the food and culture. The small farming towns I drove through on my journey across Texas made me feel like I was from another country. Much of it felt foreign, although Austin had a sense of familiarity. There are a few legendary barbecue places there, and I was excited to try some authentic, world-famous brisket. Mouth-watering with expectation, I can't tell you how disappointing it was to learn each famous restaurant was shut down. The restaurants that usually have lines longer than theme parks closed their doors to quarantine. So, instead, I took a walk down historic Sixth Street. I had been told this was the place to go to listen to music and have a fun night out. As I pulled up, parked, and got out of my car, there were only a few people walking around. Again, every building was boarded up with cleverly decorated plywood. Not one restaurant was visibly open. No bars. No music. Even though there was nothing to do, I loved just walking the streets. I kept walking throughout downtown, past the freeway underpass where many homeless people had built a small tent village. That not only reminded me of the cities back in California but that I, too, did not have a place to call home. I felt thankful to be traveling and staying in hotels that my client was covering the bill for. My time in Austin was only one night. Leaving the next morning, I managed to find a drive-through barbecue spot open that was still better than any in California.

Making it into New Orleans was surreal. I have never felt so alone, and to my surprise, I actually liked it. The city was a complete ghost town. Nearly every business was shut down and boarded up; no one was leaving their homes. Other cities I visited at least had people wandering around or the occasional restaurant open. I walked around the French Quarter, taking more photos of plywood murals, and experienced Bourbon Street with not one soul in sight. The gas lamps still kindled, and it was so quiet I could hear my own footsteps as I wandered the Quarter. New Orleans was one of my favorite cities to visit for the food. Beignets, gumbo, and jambalaya were some of my favorites that I would go out of my way for on any visit. I continued walking around and taking photos of this desolate place and saw a faint light up ahead with the quiet sound of music playing. Normally, in

New Orleans, this is to be expected everywhere, but now it was a shock. And there was a welcomed surprise—a po'boy shop was open! They were taking orders through a plywood board with a hole cut out of it. I rang the bell for service, and someone from inside yelled, "What you want, hunny?" "A shrimp po'boy, everything on it, ma'am," I replied. I leaned on the wall of the building, waiting for my order, and was so excited for some actual local food. Until this glorious stop, I was eating mostly drive-through since it was the only thing open. Even if the food was not good, it would have been perfect for the moment.

Walking out in nature, you expect to be alone, and isolation feels peaceful. But to walk around a city that really doesn't sleep and see absolutely no one is perhaps the epitome of loneliness. Speaking to the hotel staff when I returned from my walk, I mentioned, "I have never seen a place so empty. I did not see one person throughout the entire French Quarter!" "Ever since Hurricane Katrina, we have learned to lock it down," the hotel employee exclaimed. "We were locked down for a long time. We are a hardy people. We have become used to this type of thing. Hurricane or a pandemic, it's all the same procedure."

At this point in my journey, I began to enjoy my own company for the first time. What a monumental moment! My solo travels to just escape were beginning to transform me. The feelings of rejection, unworthiness, and shame were being replaced by the realization that I enjoy my own company and find value in myself. I didn't need the approval of someone else to make me feel like I was living a life of value. To find wholeness and to honestly love and respect myself was something that was quite new and transformative.

Swim Out Of The Current, And Then To Shore

Driving down the highway into Florida, I was directed off the main road-way into a checkpoint with armed guards and was feeling quite unnerved.

"State your business," the sheriff said with a stern and unshakable tough guy face.

"I'm traveling here for work, officer," I said, trying to look confident. I handed him my California ID (this gets eye rolls around the country) and told him the work that I needed to perform on my visit. He went over my official business documents and informed me I was from a high-risk Covid state and was not allowed to enter.

"Officer, I have not been there in months. I have been traveling for my client across the country and no longer have residence in California."

With a puzzled look, he glared at me and said, "Whatever, you may pass." I didn't want to say one more word, so "thank you" didn't even cross my lips. I just pressed on the accelerator and hurried along before he could change his mind. Early on in the pandemic, things were not yet politicized, and I had no idea what to expect anywhere.

It was also my first visit through the panhandle of Florida, and again, it felt like another world. Large boosted pickup trucks with neon lights on the tires seemed to be nearly everywhere. One local referred to the area as the "Redneck Riviera," which made me smile. Despite the security checkpoint to get into the state, things seemed more business as usual here.

I had family in Florida, as almost everyone who was raised in Wisconsin does, but I couldn't even visit them because of the unknowns of the pandemic. I arrived in Ft. Lauderdale, and a few days of work later, I stumbled on something that I had not seen in a while. Everything was open. I had been on the road for roughly three months. Nearly every state until this point had everything closed down or for takeout only. I badly craved a normal moment. It had been three months since I had actually eaten at a restaurant. To wander into a socially distanced bar felt like the nightcap to my journey of transformation. I enjoyed tacos, mojitos, and an unlimited supply of chips and salsa, and I had a moment of normalcy in a world that was completely chaotic in a time of paradoxical transformation in my life. I was sitting there, six feet apart from everyone, wondering if I would ever have a normal life again.

On my drive back to California, I reflected on the trip and how far I had gone. It was not just the countless miles, but also the experiences that few others would have gotten to encounter. I knew that I just traveled through one of the strangest times in world history, completely alone, while going through the most difficult time of my life. Reflecting on the trip and knowing that I had a great time all by myself gave me such profound hope that I knew I would be okay, no matter what life would bring next. I had successfully broken out of the rip current and swam back to safety.

JASON FUERSTENBERG

Jason Fuerstenberg is a first-time author living nomadically in California. Traveling regularly for clients in the coffee industry, Jason has created an unconventional yet exciting career and life on the road. During his travels, he is always looking for the best coffee, food, and opportunities to use his camera.

In his first published writing, Jason shares his experiences traveling as an essential worker at the height of the pandemic shutdowns during a time of great transition in his life.

Instagram: www.instagram.com/driftlessone/

Facebook: www.facebook.com/profile.php?id=100086579063733

3

Peace and Love

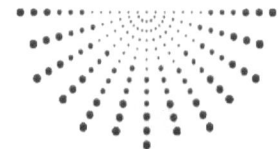

MICHELLE SAVAGE

Traveling with a lover or a friend infuses your relationship with new energy, fresh adventures, and shared stories you can retell each other when your lives fall back into a boring, monotonous pattern. Years later, you'll be crafting your kid's five thousandth PB&J and will wistfully say, "Remember that time when we rode camels in Egypt, or threw up sushi in Kyoto, or got bumped up to first class and sat next to Sting, or..." (fill in the blank with some remarkable excursion you vaguely recall but left you with a faint recollection of what freedom feels like). It's nice to have a companion and witness to your most treasured memories.

The downside of traveling with other people is that you experience a new place through the filter of your old relationship. You find yourself asking, what do *we* want to do? Where do *we* want to eat? What do *we* think about the homeless situation or that pervy guy on the train or the quality of the sheets at the hotel? Even if you're not pathetically codependent, your experience is sheltered by the fact that you can rely on each other to be on the lookout for stranger danger or find the right subway line or decipher an insult in a language neither of you bothered to learn. Two heads are better than one, and all that.

When traveling alone, you must rely on yourself to navigate your environment and relate to the strangers in it. *You* get to decide where to go and how long to stay and what *you* want to eat and how long *you* want to stare at a painting before you get bored and head to the local pub to get drunk and try eavesdropping in a language *you* didn't bother to learn. It was this second kind of travel I craved the most—to see what I was made of, to experience new things through my own filters, and more than anything, to do it alone.

When I announced to my parents at nineteen that I was going to NYC to attend a dance workshop with two of my other dancer friends, they were excited for me but said things like, "New York is so dangerous. I hope you girls stick together." They were far less enthusiastic about my plan to ditch my friends when the workshop ended and travel to Spain by myself for two weeks. I had it all figured out, though. I'd purchased a round-trip ticket from NYC to Madrid, bought a Eurail pass, got myself a shiny new passport, and had just finished taking Spanish Dos at the community college. How much more prepared could I be?

My plan was to fly into and out of Madrid and figure the rest out after I got there. I didn't book any rooms ahead of time, but I had a guidebook that listed all the youth hostels. Instead of carrying one of those two-ton backpacks that scream, "I'm a tourist!" I decided I could make it for two weeks with a regular-sized backpack, the kind you use for school books. The contents of said backpack were as follows: one blue floral sundress, two pairs of army green shorts, three tank tops (two black, one red), a black miniskirt, a burgundy cardigan sweater, black sandals, sneakers, seven pairs of underwear, a bra, toothbrush, toothpaste, a comb, pomade, a bar of soap, a bottle of lavender lotion, and a disposable camera.

Items I did not bring but probably should have: socks (my sneakers became unbearably smelly from wearing them barefoot) and a razor (by the end of the first week, I'd grown a winter pelt).

What I wanted to avoid most of all was letting on I was an American. I knew what socially sophisticated Europeans thought of American tourists—all loud and brash, wearing matching windsuits and T-shirts with the Eiffel Tower puffy painted on the front. Bellowing for all to hear about the cars that are too small, the buildings that are too old, and how rude that waiter was at dinner last night. *He didn't even try to understand English. At least here, we don't have to tip*!

I was happy that my army shorts, cropped pixie haircut buzzed close on the sides, and earnest, though failing, attempt to speak Spanish partially disguised my American identity. But now that I think of it, with my wooly legs and shoe stench, it's possible no country would claim me.

After landing in Madrid, I found an open cab where I said to the driver, "Yo voy a La Plaza Mayor, por favor." Having rehearsed this line so I could say it with enough confidence to hopefully avoid any funny business, I slid into the backseat of a car with a driver I'd never met in a city where I was so clueless that he could have driven me to Portugal, and I wouldn't have known the difference. If only my Swiss Army knife had not been confiscated at the airport, I could have snipped his eyes out with tiny nail clippers if things got sketchy.

To my relief, I was delivered to a beautiful plaza in the center of Madrid, where sixteenth-century Renaissance architecture and sidewalk cafes framed the square. The historical significance was difficult to absorb all at once, and while I was keen to explore, I was also exhausted. My guidebook mentioned a nice pension not far from there, and with the jet lag of a six-hour time difference, I made securing a place to sleep my first priority. Lucky for me, I got a room of my own. Unfortunately, three extremely intoxicated and, therefore, noisy German men occupied the room next to mine. But at twenty-five dollars a night, I could hardly complain.

For two days, I wandered around the city, getting lost, looking at monuments, and eating bocadillos from street vendors. I was having fun, but I also didn't really know what to do with myself. Independence and indecision are a troublesome pair. For the first time in my life, I was the one who had to decide where to go and navigate how to get there, and I was the one who had to ask for directions in a language I barely knew. I had wanted to travel alone for the thrill of it, to be unfettered by anyone else's ideas or opinions. I longed for a feeling of freedom and adventure, and beyond the fear of something bad happening to me, I was most afraid of squandering this precious opportunity.

The productive American part of me worried I was wasting my time, a once-in-a-lifetime experience, and should be doing or seeing more. However, I soon realized that not having a real plan meant I wasn't late for anything. It took those first days of wandering to get my "sea legs," to get used to going where the wind or my whims would take me.

By day, I walked mile after mile to cover as much ground as possible. Interested in seeing the city beyond the guidebook, I strolled through the side streets, dipping in and out of small neighborhood shops and parks.

At night, my whim was to find a bar that wasn't brightly lit inside, which, apparently, is a hard thing to do in Madrid. Who in the world wants to get sloshed under an interrogation light? In America, bars are just bright enough to find your drink but dark enough to get handsy with your date.

In spite of its magnificent arches and spires, statues, museums, and bars that are lit like the inside of a McDonald's, the vibe in Madrid was a bit formal, if not a little dull, and I felt like I was a kid at the grown-up's table. The city is like a living museum, and I wondered how long I should pretend to be rapt with the view before moving on. Flipping through my guidebook at the darkest bar in Madrid, incidentally, an Irish bar that served room-temperature Guinness, I chose my next destination.

· · · ● · ● · ● · ·

Boarding a train to Barcelona, I discovered the pro travel tip of taking night trains. If you pay a little extra for a sleeper car, you can sack out in one city and wake up in another, halfway across the country without wasting a day of travel. This felt like outsmarting my non-existent itinerary to maximize my trip.

For as long as I can remember, I've been prone to motion sickness. It happens anytime I get jostled around and I can't see where I'm going. When a train agent came into my room and saw me trying to open the window in the stuffy sleeper car, he barked at me to stop. Thankfully, when I mimed that I was going to puke, he had mercy and lowered the window about an inch. I climbed to the top bunk to suck in the fresh air and watched the Spanish sun setting over the countryside until I was sleepier than I was nauseous.

At six in the morning, I arrived in Barcelona and was greeted by blue morning skies, sunshine, and a café that served Belgian waffles topped with strawberries and whipped cream. Already, I was digging the vibrancy of this city, but how could I not love a place where most meals are a collection of small plates full of my favorite salty snacks, and the entire city shuts down each afternoon for a collective nap?

As luck would have it, I met another solo traveler, a woman from Australia named Mary, who invited me to tag along to the Picasso Museum, the Gaudi Cathedral, and a day trip to Monserrat, a monastery only accessible by a cable car at the top of a mountain. Mary had a broad smile and an air of confidence that made her a fun companion, and Mary was only the first of many strangers who would become friends. If I'd been traveling with a friend from the States, there's no way I would have made the effort to connect with so many people I didn't know.

The day Mary left, I took myself to a late-night dinner in a bustling outdoor café. As I sat alone sipping my wine and people-watching, I overheard a group of Americans a few tables over. One of them, the cute one, noticed me and asked me to join them. *Don't mind if I do!*

After another glass of wine, I walked with the mixed group of about six guys and girls down to the water. I'd already spent a few hours sunning myself by the sea earlier that afternoon, but the moon over the water at night was particularly stunning. It wasn't my idea, but when someone shouted that we should all go skinny-dipping, I also wasn't the last one to shimmy out of my clothes and run toward the water. It didn't even occur to me to feel shy or care what anyone thought. Swimming naked in the moonlight is no small luxury and one that should be enjoyed.

Back on the beach and back in my clothes, the cute one sat next to me, and after we talked for a bit, he leaned over and kissed me. Breaking away from the group, we spent the rest of the night strolling along the city streets and finally popped into a bar for a last nightcap. When I told him it was time for me to get some sleep, he walked me back to my pension and said goodnight. Satisfied with my evening, I slipped out of my sandals and began repacking my backpack, but before I could finish, there was a banging on my door. I opened it to find the cute one looking anxious and apologetic. He had been locked out of his room and wondered if he could stay with me.

I said he could and thought, *I hope this guy doesn't think he's getting any tonight,* but to my surprise, he was the one who crumbled over the guilt of our previous kiss and confessed he had a girlfriend back home. *Oh, boy...here we go.*

The poor guy was in knots about it, which, for some reason, struck me as hilarious. Feeling truly uncomplicated about my Euro-fling, I laughed and said, "Dude, we're good. Just go to sleep." The night had been a fun little romance, but truth be told, the cute one wasn't my type back in the real world. He was too preppy and too young (because he was my age). Not to mention, I'd just learned that he's the kind of guy willing to cheat on his girlfriend. *No, gracias!* Shortly after he drifted off to sleep, I finished packing my bag and left him lying in my bed as I tip-toed out into the morning light. It was time to hit the road.

· · · · ●· ●· · ·

I'd never planned on going to Paris. I hadn't purchased a Parisian map, let alone a whole guidebook, and only knew how to say "yes, no, please, thank you, and my name is" in French. I also remembered the word for bathing suit—maillot—but wasn't sure how helpful it would be.

Hopping off the train, I spotted a kid with a giant backpack and asked him if I could look at the map he was holding. Turns out his name was Phil, and he was also from the US. Unlike me, Phil was traveling with another young couple and was meeting up with them later at a youth hostel called the Peace and Love. Happy to have a recommendation on where to stay, I followed Phil to the Peace and Love, where I discovered that the downstairs of the hostel housed a cool bar with nightly live music.

The rooms were co-ed and housed multiple bunk beds, and since I didn't know anyone else, Phil agreed to be my bunkmate. Not only did he appear harmless, but I was bigger than him, and after a two-week dance intensive in New York, my legs could crush coconuts. Good thing I was feeling strong; our room was on the top floor of what turned out to be a fourteen-floor walk-up. With that many stairs between my room and the ground floor, I had to carefully calculate what I needed to take with me for the day before leaving. Running back up to grab a forgotten sweater or some sunglasses would cost me an extra thirty minutes and 1,200 calories.

The lounge of the Peace and Love was a Petri dish for young travelers to meet and hang out. Jackie was a raver girl from Arizona who was a year younger than me and was also traveling by herself. She was tough, funny, and had a chip on her shoulder, so I liked her right away. Nate was from New York, a film student who planned to hop around Europe for as long as possible until his funds ran out. I was immediately attracted to his salty humor and thick New York accent. I thought *this is the kind of guy I'd like to bring back to the real world,* but his eyes were on Jackie from the start. After a night of drinking in the lounge, a group of us decided we'd travel to the Palace of Versailles the next day.

Our first train delivered us to a suburb at least an hour from the city's center, and it took only a moment to figure out we were nowhere near a fancy French chateau. I guess two heads are only better than one if one of those heads can accurately read the metro map. We spent all afternoon waiting for another train to travel back to where we began, course correct-ed, and finally arrived at the Palace of Versailles. Stepping onto the palace grounds, I was gobsmacked by the intricately manicured gardens radiating from the palace in all directions. Unfortunately for us, it was almost closing time, but tour officials generously let us in for an abbreviated visit. It was breathtaking, each architectural detail hand-carved, gilded in gold, and accessorized with crystal chandeliers dangling from high above. Versailles was so majestic that even our short stay was worth the trouble it took getting there.

As we exited the palace, dark clouds accumulated above us, and it started sprinkling. A thick crowd of palace visitors already waiting for the bus to head back to the metro meant we would be waiting a while for our turn. The rain came down harder, filling the gutters that spilled over our feet. Our group huddled together under the single umbrella brought by someone who traveled with a larger backpack than I did.

When it was finally our turn to board a bus, our soaked clothes clung to our shivering bodies, and I was feeling the length of the day. Relaxing into the sticky vinyl seats, we took solace in the rumbling of the bus engine and the repetitive squeak of the wiper blades. I didn't mind that it was crowded or that the air was thick, so long as we had a ride going in the right direction. I closed my eyes, feeling thankful we'd made it.

It wasn't but a few minutes, though, before the bus stopped. Looking out the windows, I saw cars floating in the streets. Water was now seeping into the bottom of the bus, and with that, the driver opened the door and told us all to get off and walk the rest of the way.

My mind raced with thoughts like...*Um, excuse me? What is going on here? Don't you know I'm an American? In my country, we don't throw people off buses in the middle of a typhoon or whatever you call this God-forsaken storm. We call in the National Guard or the Army Reserves or Texans with boats to save the women and children.*

Clearly, I was still on the border between the two—woman and child—and my inner American was showing. Together, my new friends and I waded through the water, holding hands, following sidewalks with the highest elevation until we finally found the metro and rode in silence back to the Peace and Love.

That night, as drinks flowed and a band played so loudly that we couldn't even yell at each other over the music, I felt a deep weariness settle into my body. No amount of rallying could keep me from an early bedtime, so I said goodnight to my friends and climbed the thirteen steep flights of stairs to my room. Paris was kicking my ass, and I needed to sleep.

Collapsing onto the top bunk, I mused over how much had already happened in the week since I'd landed in Madrid. I thought of the relative nature of time and how quickly a week can pass at home when I'm stuck in a routine, but a week of travel can feel like a month. The door to my room opened and closed behind a man I didn't know. I'd seen him sitting in the corner of the lounge the night before, but he was much older than everyone else there, so I didn't imagine he was a guest, let alone my new bunkmate. Until now, it was just Phil and I in our room.

Without saying a word, the man climbed into the bunk below mine, and within minutes, I heard heavy breathing as the metal bed frame shook in a rhythmic motion. I froze, afraid to breathe or open my eyes. This asshole was jerking off, and I was at the top of a tower, only accessible by a thousand stairs. And with a band blaring on the bottom floor, there'd be no one to hear me scream. I thought of making a run for it, but the door was opposite the bunk, and the room was small enough for him to grab me before I could open it. Instead, I stayed perfectly still. Waiting. Waiting for an eternity. Waiting for him to finish. Waiting for him to try climbing on top of me. Suddenly feeling zero confidence in my coconut-crushing strength, I waited to see if I'd have to fight against a man twice my size.

And then...wham!

The door to our room swung open. It was Phil coming to check on me and see if I wanted to hang out. I flew off the top bunk, slid on my shoes, grabbed my backpack along with a few loose belongings, and was out the door in seconds. I never once looked down at the bottom bunk, afraid of what I'd see, though Phil reported the jacker-offer just pretended to be asleep.

Phil's grand entrance was nothing less than a real-life miracle. Then again, it also seems like a word problem you'd learn in Sunday school. *So, class, how many guardian angels does it take to drag a full-grown fella* up *thirteen flights of stairs just to check on someone he hardly knows?* My answer: I have no idea, but thank you God for sending me a rescuer in the form of a kind kid named Phil. So much for being solo; apparently, I traveled with an angelic entourage.

After reporting the incident to the front desk and securing another bunk in a room with Jackie and a bunch of other people I didn't know, I decided to hang out with Jackie and Nate. I was too shaken up to sleep, so we took a walk up the street to sit by the grotto. It was late by then, probably one in the morning, and the night air felt milky on my skin. Nate's antics kept Jackie and me laughing, and their flirting was subtle enough that I didn't feel like a third wheel. Wanting to explore, Nate dropped down the twenty or so feet into the concrete grotto below while Jackie and I hung out curbside.

Nate was only gone a minute when two large men in their early twenties appeared out of the subway and headed straight for us. They were drunk and looking for a good time. I was sober and had already spent my night trying to avoid that kind of good time. They did their best to proposition us in French, and this time, Jackie took the lead in telling them to go away. Since no means no in both languages and they weren't leaving, things started feeling more tense. Jackie, who'd had a fair amount to drink that night, began yelling at them to, as she delicately put it, "Get the fuck away from us!" The larger of the two men took a step closer to her, and she shoved him back with both hands, to which he responded with a right hook straight to her nose. Blood sprayed from her face, and the two men bolted back down the subway stairwell. Once back at the hostel, the front desk guy gave Jackie an ice pack for her nose and a joint for her feelings, which I thought was pretty good customer service. Peace and Love, indeed.

Jackie returned to the States the next day, and although my crush on Nate only increased the more time I spent with him, it turned out we were also fantastic travel partners. We visited the Eiffel Tower and the Louvre, and with just five days left before I needed to be back in Madrid, we decided we'd had enough of Paris and headed to San Sebastian in the Basque country of Spain. After stocking up on French wine and snacks, we sat up most of the night on the train, talking and drinking wine from the bottle.

San Sebastian seemed like a welcome dream after the chaos in Paris. The city is a teardrop of fine architecture, fine dining, and luxury shopping wedged between the sea and the Pyrenees Mountains. I could have lived there for the rest of my life and died happily. It was in San Sebastian that I bought a beautiful pair of Spanish leather sandals and threw my disgusting sneakers in the garbage. I bought a razor and shaved my legs and put on my black skirt and red tank top for the first time during the journey. In part, sprucing myself up was a last-ditch effort to capture Nate's attention, but it also felt amazing just to unearth my lady legs and go out to a nice dinner.

Alone with Nate, I hoped things would be different. As we took in the sites, we shared an easy banter and made each other laugh. We discussed the movies he planned to make, and we snapped photos of each other with our disposable cameras. I kept waiting and hoping Nate would make a move, but he never did. I guess I wasn't his type in the real world.

My solo train ride back to Madrid was a day trip from San Sebastian, and with as many experiences as I'd packed into a two-week trip, I was fine spending a day of it sitting down and looking out the window. The two weeks I'd spent dancing in New York seemed like eons ago.

Being dazzled and mesmerized, in shock and in awe, and often a little scared showed me who I am at my core and also molded parts of me into something new. Traveling alone sharpened my ability to look out for myself, increased my tolerance for discomfort, and helped me become more discerning. I developed a thirst for more unscripted experiences, and I suddenly wanted more—more out of life, more travel, more of the thing that feels like freedom. There was no stuffing this genie back into the bottle. Still, I was ready to go home for a bit.

Ah, *home*, I thought as I watched the landscape pass by my window. The idea of sleeping in my own bed after crashing in half a dozen rickety bunk beds started sounding pretty wonderful, as did eating a giant American cheeseburger and sipping drinks with ice in them. I suddenly couldn't wait to see my friends again and to drive my car all around a city where I wouldn't get lost.

Sitting across from me in my train car was a father and son from Morocco, eating colorful, fragrant foods from tins with delightful spice combinations my nose could not decipher. I was enchanted by the father's tenderness with his son and discovered he spoke a bit of English. He introduced himself and asked me where I was from. When I told him I was from the United States, his eyes lit up, and he said, "Oh yes, Bill Clinton and Monica Lewinsky!"

I smiled sheepishly, thinking *oh, great...this is what stands out to you about the United States*. It was 1998, and the scandal was all over the news at home, but I hadn't realized how far news like that travels. And then, to clarify further, I said, "Well, really, I'm from Texas," to which he enthusiastically responded, "Like *Dallas*, the TV show?"

After a brief pause, I sighed and smiled at him, "Yeah, like *Dallas*, the TV show. I'm an American."

MICHELLE SAVAGE

Michelle Savage is an international best-selling author, speaker, and publisher. In 2022, Michelle founded Sulit Press, a boutique publishing house based in Austin, Texas. Through Sulit's Concierge Publishing Package, Multi-Author Book Program, and Manuscript Mastermind, Michelle has already helped dozens of aspiring writers become published authors. She believes everyone has a story to tell and that the way we connect, learn, and build empathy for one another is to write and share those stories.

Website: www.sulitpress.com

Instagram: www.instagram.com/sulitpressbooks/

Facebook: www.facebook.com/SulitPress

LinkedIn: www.linkedin.com/in/michelle-savage-43032659/

4

Life as a Life-Long Nomad

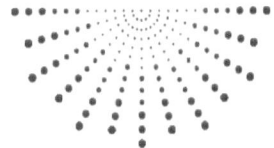

VINCENT MCNEELEY

"Where are you from?" he asked. Should I tell him I'm from the desert...? From a place nestled in the embrace of barren mountains and swept by azure skies—a place where silence carries the whispers of ancient tales, and the air, crisp and clear, hangs heavy with the scent of sage and juniper. Sunsets are a spectacle here, casting the vast expanses in a blush of colors—hues of fiery oranges, dusky purples, and molten golds all meld into a symphony that captivates the senses.

By day, the sun soaks the desert in an unyielding glow, illuminating the muted palette of the landscape, setting alight the sands with a shimmering gold. The solitude is profound, interrupted only by the occasional rustling of hidden creatures and the distant cries of hawks soaring in the cobalt expanse above.

When night falls, the high desert transforms into an amphitheater of cosmic wonder. A velvet shroud speckled with countless stars drapes the terrain, the Milky Way painting a streak of celestial magic across the heavens. The desert becomes a stage for the moon's soft glow to trace silhouettes and play with shadows, an ethereal dance of light and dark.

Living in the high desert is living within a waking dream—one that seamlessly blends the stark reality of survival with the mesmerizing beauty of a world stripped to its bare essentials. It is an experience of living within a masterpiece—raw, untamed, beautifully desolate—a place that invites contemplation, discovery, and an undeniable sense of awe.

No, I thought, *I can not tell him that.* This was yet a dream. How about the Pacific...? Along the Southern California coastline, where the frothy waves of the cerulean sea meet a ribbon of golden sand, hemmed in by rugged cliffs and swaying palms. With a sun that perpetually bathes the landscape, this coastal haven exudes an aura of eternal summer. Up and down the coast, rolling hills of wildflowers drift in the breeze. Luxuriant flora thrives here, from the brilliantly-hued bougainvillea climbing over terracotta walls to the tall, majestic palm trees that line the boulevards, their fronds gently swaying against the backdrop of a cloudless blue sky. Succulents and wildflowers dot the dunes, adding splashes of vibrant color to the sun-bleached landscape.

Nope, that is a lie. I traveled there once for a family vacation, but I can not say that either. I do not live there, yet. My most exciting views, up to this point, were just in my dreams. I spent lots of time flipping through magazines, browsing the internet, and watching shows of all the places in the country I wanted to travel to. Traveling the world seemed like a distant pipe dream, since I was living in middle America, so I mostly had my sights set on travel within the country. I wanted to tell these profound stories of my exhilarating travels to this amazing man in the hopes that he would become my lifetime adventure partner. My travels, up to this point, had not been as adventurous.

Where was I from, he asked. Cleveland, Ohio, I answered. I was born in Cleveland. You might be laughing at the juxtaposition of Cleveland and the ethereal southern coast or high desert that live rent-free in my head. But Cleveland does have some amazing attractions. The Cleveland Metroparks and the Rock and Roll Hall of Fame are great. Despite the lack of an ocean, Lake Erie is quite nice, too. But on a dating app like Tinder, and talking to gay guys who live in warm southern climates, Cleveland is still a tough sell.

I was new to talking to guys, new to dating, and new to exploring my sexuality. I hesitated to tell him where I am really from, because I have never really felt at home anywhere. When you are traveling all the time, where you are from becomes less relevant than the memories you have made along the way. Traveling from the bustling suburbia of Ohio to the thriving corn fields of Kansas as a child, my life had taken me to many places in the Midwest. These were not exactly the most glamorous places to describe, but I learned a lot from these adventures at an early age.

Even as a child, there are two constants in my life: being a lifelong nomad and always taking a new path. I was always the "new kid" when I was in school. This was an experience I repeated twelve times as I switched schools due to my dad's career. He worked in multimedia production, traveling the country setting up production studios for various business entities that would then broadcast content around the world. In school, I befriended my teachers because I was adapting to an ever-changing curriculum, and in some instances, quite literally learning different accounts of history. This was a hard adaptation to overcome, depending on how ahead or behind I was in a given subject. But, adapting to change is something I gravitated toward as it eventually began to feel more comfortable and necessary.

I was about to make the biggest change of my adult life, changing to embrace who I really was with a guy I had chatted with for a while on Tinder after having gone on a few dates with other guys. I wanted him to be my boyfriend. On our first date, we went hiking along the Chattahoochee River, just a few minutes north of Atlanta, a place I called home after college as I started my career in tech. For twenty-five years, I lived "in the closet." Growing up in schools in the Midwest, I never met another LBGTQ+ student. Kids in school used the word "gay" to describe anything that was not good when making fun of each other. So, I internalized being gay as being bad. Now, I finally had someone who I loved, who was "out," and who wanted me to come out as well. He made me feel comfortable in my own skin, supported my passions, and gave me hope for the future.

While growing up, I saw all my friends going on dates, spending time with people of the opposite sex. It was a heteronormative nightmare to dance the fine line between the facade of being a shy kid with the reality of being too scared to ever ask another guy out on a date for fear I would be ridiculed beyond measure. I spent those years conceding that I may not find true love and all the joys that come with it. Finally finding someone with whom I could share this joy changed my whole outlook on life and the future I wanted to live. I felt a sense of purpose to embrace authenticity in every aspect of my life, leaning into my truest self. One that is courageous, curious, and more confident. Suddenly, I wanted to embrace all the fears

I had held on for so long: showing up authentically as a gay man, dating, exploring nomadically, and embracing my strengths wholeheartedly.

It was time, time to be myself. No longer was I trapped in tiny rural towns in Kansas, Alabama, or Ohio. I was in the rainbow capital of the South, Atlanta, working for a company headquartered in California with a gay boyfriend for the first time in my life. I came out on Instagram. In a moment of catharsis, after our second date (my birthday), I decided to rip off the bandaid that had been on for twenty-five years: I posted a picture of us together on Instagram. I did not specifically call attention to this picture, the fact I had a boyfriend, or say the words, "I am gay." Instead, I opened the door to posting more pictures together and set my life in a new direction. My family and friends quickly noticed and embraced me with open arms. I started growing out my hair, something I dreamed about doing but also feared doing most of my teenage years. Now that I could be myself without worrying about what others thought about me, nearly twenty-five years of anxiety and stress suddenly vanished in an instant.

The direction—that would change as we continued to go on adventures together, traveling to Savannah, Chicago, and Los Angeles. I was living the dream, exploring all the places I had wanted to visit. I quickly realized what made my adventures special as an adult was not the places I visited, but who I visited them with. I was making memories with a great adventure partner, and it felt amazing. In the span of two years, we visited more than ten states. We wanted to explore more, and things were beginning to feel a bit cramped, given that the pandemic had put us together in an 800-square-foot apartment for many more hours each day than before. We had been given the opportunity to work remotely, and we seized it to travel to Utah.

I found an Airbnb in Logan, Utah, to stay in for six months. I quick-ly became friends with the owners as I saw them more than I saw my boyfriend, who took a job in wildlife conservation. Utah was my high desert dream; only instead of the sandy mesas, we chose the mountains. They were spectacularly beautiful, but since we were visiting in the fall, this beauty quickly became beautifully cold as well. As the cold moved in, the cold shoulder did, too.

My boyfriend and I had been together for over two years, but we were slowly drifting apart. At a rave my Airbnb hosts were throwing around Halloween, I shared my relationship challenges with my host and learned that he was also going through some challenges. We bonded deeply, and I learned the true value of friendship as an adult. I would leave this Airbnb and my new friends, just as I had to do in childhood. Only this time, I was living in the future, and I knew technology would keep us in touch in ways my childhood self could have only imagined.

My boyfriend and I traveled back to Atlanta and decided that we wanted to commit to living on the road full-time in the most literal sense, as we packed up our apartment into a storage unit and built out both of our Jeeps to live in next. Thinking our adventures in nature would help give us both the space and serenity we needed to mend our differences and revive our relationship, we embarked on this new stage in our journey. As I worked during the day, he helped pack, plan, and search for other work opportunities to support our future traveling lifestyle. We spent the winter holiday convincing our families of our grand plans, of which they were more than skeptical. We planned to go back to Utah after he found another opportunity in conservation. We started to prepare for the move, and with some of the woodworking skills I picked up in rural Kansas, we created the comforts of a home on four wheels.

A bed, a kitchen, a pantry, and an office. I had everything I needed to work, live, and explore our new "home base" of Kanab, Utah, while my boyfriend was on his eight-day on, four-day off conservation assignments in the field. At least, that was until my first night in the middle of winter living in a soft-top Jeep Wrangler. It was the desert, but it was not the summer oasis desert I described earlier. It was the winter wonderland of deserts. I was freezing and discouraged and never wanted to be at the beach more than that moment. As I let out each breath, I could see the condensation in front of my eyes. I rolled up in my blanket and tried to sleep.

The next morning, I turned on my laptop to start my workday, and nothing happened. I feared I had broken it and was no less than four hours from the closest Apple repair shop. I had no clue what was happening; all I knew was I could see my breath, and I had made all the wrong decisions. At that moment, I did not want to adapt, I wanted to quit. I wanted to go back to my warm apartment and cozy bed. But, I did not have a warm apartment or cozy bed to go back to. I was lying in it, and it was neither warm nor cozy. After a while, my car finally started to warm up, and just like me, my laptop finally came to life.

This chill, sleep, freeze, repeat cycle continued for several days. Some days, I managed ok. Other days, I gave in and bought a hotel room. When I capitulate to Mother Nature, my boyfriend, having just arrived from a tent-camping experience in the wilderness on his assignments, would not be sympathetic to my struggles in the way I hoped. "We do not need another hotel room," he would say. "I can not stay in the snow again...another night in a row," I replied. I wanted to be close to him, but living in the wintery wonderland of Utah without a warm place to escape to was not working. The idea of saving money living in my car turned into spending money living on the road. I decided Jeeps were good for exploring, but not living full-time.

So, I bought a camper. Just like the trains I used to watch in the rail yard with my dad when I was a kid, I knew the little caboose of a camper I pulled behind my Jeep would give me many creature comforts of a home away from home. Yet, I was home. I was home for the first time in my life. Living the joyous, free-spirited adventure I had always imagined.

The joy of this adventure would never fade, even though my and my partner's love for each other did. It was a dark, starry night, and I was alone in my camper. We had taken a trip to Colorado to explore, and on the drive back to Utah, we stopped for a hike. That was the last hike we took together as a couple as we broke up by the end of it. We arrived back in town, and I was quickly taken back to being the new kid and not knowing a single person in the place I lived. All the anxiety, fear, and trauma of childhood resurfaced. I felt alone. I was still in Southern Utah, with one friend a few hours away. Not wanting to concede as a failure to my family, who had tepidly embraced my Jeep-life antics. Not wanting to go back to living in a crowded city five minutes down the street from my office. And not wanting to quit exploring. I decided to drive to my friend's house in Page, Arizona, that night.

I never appreciated showers more than I did while visiting him. I had a shower in my camper, but I couldn't take the long, relaxing showers I desired. The logistics of filling a water tank, dumping the tank, charging an inverter with enough solar power so you can power the camper with all your electronics and a water heater took all the relaxation out of showering. I still tried to take short showers at his house, feeling guilty for the declining water levels I saw in his backyard every day. He lived on Lake Powell.

Driving through this part of the county, I came to realize the negative effects of human civilization on our ecosystems. Much of this land is Navajo, and from the paintings on the reservation buildings, you quickly see all the ways man had been at odds with nature. It was not long before my visit to this area that the Navajo had won a long battle to close a coal-powered electric plant on the Colorado River. One that had polluted the population but not broken their spirit. It was a part of history that I was seeing and hearing from firsthand accounts for the first time in my life.

Growing up in Kansas for a large portion of my life, I learned a lot about the Trail of Tears in school. But, much of the history I was taught about the event was white-washed with generalizations and brevity. I never learned that after moving indigenous people from their ancestral lands to the Midwest and western United States, generations of indigenous people would continue to suffer in the pursuit of extracting the lands for all they have to offer. Back in the time of the Manhattan Project, many indigenous families worked to mine uranium—the sludgy radioactive byproduct that is still being cleaned up along the banks of the very same Colorado River, just north of the reservation in Moab, Utah. Generations of lives were impacted by radiation poisoning, which is still affecting families today, and cleanup efforts are still underway. I realized from these experiences that the history I learned in school as a kid was not the full history that I was seeing before my eyes.

The Colorado River, however wrought with historical tragedy, was magnificent. It ebbed and flowed like a gleaming beacon, reflecting the light of the sun on the walls of the majestic canyon it carved. I realized why this river was so special to the people here. It was a source of sustenance, entertainment, and relief from the hot sun. This heat, which starts to melt the snow in the mountains of Colorado, has continued to cause a steady decline in precipitation each year and thereby decrease the volume of the river.

I've kayaked it no less than ten times, fearing one day I might not be able to come back to it again if water levels were to get too low for recreation due to climate change. Another lesson I have now learned the hard way, make the most of every day because the next may not be the same as the last. I ended up staying with my friend in Page for a few months. Continuing to make friends on proximity-based dating apps, I hoped these friendships would lead to more adventures one day soon enough.

Not wanting to overstay my welcome with my friend, I left Arizona to travel to my dream destination, Southern California. The place I had fallen in love with as a child was also the home to one of my favorite cousins, so I decided to make a visit. This is my happy place, and given the pain I was going through with my breakup, the sadness of seeing the drastic effects of climate change firsthand, and the dichotomy of experiencing such beautiful people and nature who had been taken advantage of...I needed a little happiness.

My cousin and I went hiking along the oceanview mountainsides. We got lost together looking for babbling brooks and shared good memories of the adventures we'd had together when we were younger. And we bonded over the love we had lost in others along our journey. Southern California had been home all along, even if I did not know it. Home, at that moment, was the comfort of knowing that I had a place to exist where I felt safe, loved, and cared for.

It was the memories I made with my cousin that summer that gave me the energy to date once again, continue my nomadic adventures, pursue new friendships with others, and continue to find more ways to make lasting memories.

After the pandemic forced everyone into the comfort of their homes and workplaces began shutting down across the country, I was given confidence that I would be able to continue my adventures in perpetuity. Working as a software engineer for a company that enables other organizations across the world to support their remote workforces, my company fully embraced my nomadic lifestyle. So, I decided to create a nomad group at work, buy some new cinematography equipment, start posting my adventures on social media, and plan trips with all the new friends I had made through our new nomad group. Nearly thirty personal friendships and over 250 virtual friendships resulted in countless adventures across the country.

The next year, I traveled around the globe nearly two times in miles, establishing roots (or what I like to call "home bases") in four places: Southern California, Southern Utah, Alabama, and Georgia, with my several storage units, adventure rigs, or dwellings. I took over 30,000 pictures and hours of film across the United States. I have been given "once-in-a-lifetime opportunities" on a regular basis, and I hope to continue making the most of them each and every day.

My travels are sometimes spontaneous and sometimes planned, but one thing I can always count on is that they will bring me new joy and wisdom unlike any other experience has given me. My adventures have taken me to the high desert, the high mountains, and the high life of Southern California and continue to take me to new places all the time. I am grateful for all the friends I have met along the way and all the life my travels have given me. I am a nomad, a free-spirit, and a lifelong adventurer. My travels have and will push me outside my comfort zone, and I choose to let go of my fears. Now, those places from my dreams don't just live rent-free in my mind, I live rent-free in them.

As I write this, I just got back from Puerto Rico with my new love. He's an amazing guy who I became friends with from my travels back and forth across the country on my search for deeper meaning, love, and purpose. He has been right in my backyard this entire time. We talked for more than two years, but he was never more than two hours from me when I came back to visit my parents in Alabama.

This trip with him was special for many reasons, but most importantly, it marked his first flight and our first adventure together. As a nomad, one of my greatest joys comes from showing people all that travel has to offer. It can, and does, change you. This trip definitely changed us: it cemented our love, his love for travel, and our love together in our search for our next home together. I think we might just have another trip back to Puerto Rico in store; hopefully, we will get to stay a while longer in a little slice of paradise that is all our own, forever.

VINCENT MCNEELEY

V incent McNeeley is a Senior Technical Program Manager at VMware, where he plays a critical role in facilitating a seamless multi-cloud workspace experience for clients to enable the anywhere workspace. As the Global Co-Lead for PRIDE@VMware's Power of Difference Business Resource Group, he is an active advocate for LGBTQIA+ workforce inclusivity on a global scale. A sought-after speaker, Vincent frequently addresses crowds on subjects ranging from innovation and sustainability to artificial intelligence, all while highlighting their relevance to diversity, equity, inclusion, and belonging (DEIB) efforts. Embracing the lifestyle of a full-time digital nomad, he relishes documenting his world travels on his blog, adventureswithvincent.com.

LinkedIn: www.linkedin.com/in/vincentmcneeley/

Instagram: instagram.com/adventureswithvincent/

Website: adventureswithvincent.com

5

The Wings of Freedom

JULIE CANDELON

September 30, 2014

It's ten o'clock at night on move-in day, and my spacious two-bedroom rental suddenly feels like a tiny little shoebox. I'm sitting on the floor, exhausted and surrounded by so many boxes that I can barely move. I can feel my throat getting tight as I try not to burst into tears.

Downsizing from our family house to this single-mom apartment brings its fair share of challenges. But something else is making me emotional tonight. Was it a mistake to leave my husband? No, of course not. It doesn't cross my mind even once. We are done, I'm sure of it. However, the unknown ahead of me, the financial stress, the need to rebuild everything and raise a kid alone far away from my home country...it's all incredibly scary and overwhelming. And it's so far from the original plan! Where did my American dream go so wrong??

September 3, 2007

I'm standing outside, happily surrounded by a mountain of suitcases, trying to distract my six-month-old baby. We're jet lagged and sweating in the 100-degree heat while waiting for my husband to grab the rental car. The cat is staring at me from his travel crate. I can sense his profound resentment that piled up during the thirteen-hour flight from Paris to Los Angeles. The parking lot speakers are playing *Surfin' USA* by The Beach Boys. It's pretty surreal. I'm feeling a weird mix of exhaustion, adrenaline, and excitement. I'm taking the moment in, and I smile...this is it!

After months of meticulous planning, we packed all our belongings, left behind our lives, and immigrated to California. The decision wasn't easy to announce: I was seven months pregnant with my son when we shared our intentions. The profound impact of living far away from our family was immediately tangible. Yet, it was also impossible to pass on the opportunity. After all, I had always hoped to live in Southern California, this fun and exciting place I had learned to love as an exchange student and as a tourist with my parents.

My husband finally shows up with the car. We're on our way to San Diego, driving south from LAX. I call my parents, leaving them a voicemail mixed with hysteria and laughter. They always encouraged me to take risks and fostered my love of travel from a young age. Their entrepreneurial and adventurous spirit inspires me every day. So when my parents hear my excitement on the phone, they can only be happy and wish me the best for what is supposed to be a three- to five-year-long trip.

"Actually, the best gift you could have given her was a lifetime of adventures." —Lewis Carroll, *Alice's Adventures in Wonderland*

Luckily, I am clueless about how lost I will feel at first. Taking such a massive leap away from home is certainly a challenge. As a freshly arrived foreigner, I find myself surrounded by unknown faces. For a while, my realtor and my banker are my closest acquaintances. There isn't a single soul nearby that I can confidently trust or rely on based on prior experience. Instead, I have to place my faith in complete strangers and believe that they truly have our best interest at heart.

Merely a month after our arrival, we are caught amid a wildfire evacuation that affects over a million San Diegans. Navigating a major disaster with an infant in a foreign country is obviously stressful. But California embraces us with open arms: Countless individuals step forward to lend their inspiring support and kindness. They hold our hands and guide us through it all.

As the dust settles, I'm constantly dealing with logistical matters. What is the best laundry detergent? Explain to me credit history again. How do I buy a cell phone without an SSN? It all requires effort. And everything feels entirely new: brands, processes, expectations, and even popular culture references. I decide to embrace curiosity, be open to doing things differently, and just take it one step at a time. It is okay to ask for help and not have it all figured out right away. However, it can lead to amusing situations—like when our thick French accent confuses waiters each time we order water at a restaurant. So, after being thirsty for a while, we switch to Diet Coke until our English becomes more understandable!

On the flip side, there are also delightful surprises while immersing myself in American traditions. I have the pleasure of meeting my amazing friend Liza at a cooking class I take to prepare my first Thanksgiving dinner. We connect instantly and spend every Thanksgiving together moving forward. Our families form unbreakable bonds.

After the initial adjustment, my first few years in San Diego are like a joyful TV spot: a happy life with an adorable little French kid growing more American every day, sun-kissed skin year-round, dinners at the beach, girls' nights out, a busy career, and loved ones visiting regularly.

I quickly realize that visiting a country and living in it are two entirely distinct experiences. While the former is enjoyable, the latter is transformative. Living the day-to-day life allows me to forge meaningful connections. Embracing the nuances of American culture also deepens my understanding of the world in general and its diverse people. It creates a space for introspection, challenging my preconceived notions. Every conversation becomes an occasion to gain new insights. Every experience is a chance to learn. I notice the difference between the French, who tend to fix what's broken, and Americans, who focus on replicating what works. As we face the 2008 financial crisis, I realize cultural traits can empower people with resilience and a positive attitude.

When my son joins his first daycare, I also notice how much his education differs from what I experienced in France. We emphasize academic rigor and structure, essential learning skills, and, among other things, we cultivate a taste for varied foods. Additionally, we consider it critical to equip children with the skills needed to navigate the adult world. In contrast, my son lives in a society that primarily caters to the needs of children, which I consider both a benefit and a concern. But most importantly, he soon acquires a sense of initiative, leadership, creative thinking, and entrepreneurship unmatched in the French system. When it comes to discipline or food education, though.... The good news is that, in the end, there is no right or wrong model, just great ideas to take from both worlds. I can create my own ideal educational mix and give every chance of success to my son. There seems to be many ways to view the world and what matters.

It is probably due to their education that most Americans are not afraid to dream and dream big. And they're pretty vocal about it, too. I remember one night in 2008 at an event supporting working moms. I had expressed concerns about starting my own business. Shouldn't I understand how to establish a company before taking on any clients? The overwhelming support and encouragement I receive from these women is truly awe-inspiring. Words matter. That night, in a completely unexpected move, I decide to go for it, start my own business, and figure things out along the way. JMarketing is born!

A few months later, I share with one of these women that my husband won't let me buy a laptop until my business is thriving. Amy assures me with conviction: "We will get you on the path to making six figures in no time!" A six-figure income sounds like pure fantasy, given my much lower Parisian standards and the current economy. Yet, her complete confidence makes me want to believe. Soon enough, I reach my goals and go after new ceilings to break through. The impact of these women on me, through their simple yet profound words of encouragement, is beyond measure. It has forever altered the course of my life, and I am eternally grateful for their influence.

A couple of years later, I'm having lunch with a customer discussing hopes and goals when her husband asks me a very simple question. "What do you want your legacy to be, Julie?" Silence...I'm completely taken by surprise as I hear this question for the first time. I feel a rush of embarrassment as I realize I lack a suitable answer. I reply with a weak and simplistic "My son?...I also care a lot about the oceans, so maybe having a good impact on the environment?" That day, I vow to define a meaningful life purpose and craft its corresponding action plan. I need to impact the world positively and never feel ignorant or self-centered like that day.

These Americans are really pushing me to grow and think constantly!

> "One's destination is never a place, but a new way of seeing things." —Henry Miller

They say you choose to settle or relocate within the first five years of expatriation. Well, I'm in no rush to leave. Still, our reality isn't as picture-perfect as the San Diego ads let you believe.

If I'm being honest, the road is also paved with difficulties, and not everyone is loving the experience. I cringe every time someone asks me how much we like it here, because as much as I love everything about moving to the US, I am lying on behalf of my husband. He is having a much harder time adjusting than me. It creates misunderstandings, resentment, and an immense drift between us. We knew it coming here: More than half of expatriations end in a divorce. We even talked about it one night in Paris and vowed to prevent it from happening to us. What I didn't realize back then was that the stress and pressure of expatriation wouldn't just transform our relationship but amplify what already existed. This exciting trip is giving me a fresh perspective on my entire life, including my marriage. I now see it for what it is.

The aftermath is quite simple: a complete loss of self-confidence after years of a destructive relationship I've allowed myself to drift into. Without any long-time friends or family around to provide perspective, I lose myself. Behind closed doors, I feel worthless, confused, and doubt myself for too long. Once a joyful, optimistic, and trusting young woman, I'm now an emotional thirty-something with feelings of inferiority and emptiness. I am married, yet I have never felt lonelier in my entire life. Both professionally and personally, I am craving consideration and emotional support. I want to be seen. I ask for couples therapy; however, I'm the only one attending the sessions.

After five years in San Diego, we move to San Francisco for work, and things become even harder. To this day, I still feel like a dark cloud comes over me when I drive by our first San Francisco apartment. There, I experience that eye-opening moment of facing a health scare and realizing my husband may not be there for me in the worst circumstances. There is no coming back from the feeling of being on your own, in a foreign hospital, scared for your life.

So, I am sick, exhausted, and devastated. I become sleepless and can't avoid facing what I have been ignoring until now: My soul is slowly dying, and my marriage is over. Some say divorced couples give up too rapidly. I really took my time. But I can't give up on the idea of a better life. And my son needs to know that what he is witnessing is not a happy marriage. I need to show him life can be better.

"Freedom has no price." —my dad

The loneliness of my marriage gives way to the quietness and emptiness of my new home when my son is not around. It is deafening. I need to find comfort in being alone and rediscover myself after being lost for so long. It's tough to sit there and ask, "Who am I, and what do I want to do with my life here?" The years of my failed marriage are now behind me, but they have a lasting and defining impact on my life. They serve as the foundation for my resilience, allowing me to hit rock bottom and rise up to breathe fresh air. There is only one choice from there: start from scratch and rebuild. Being a mom, I have no other option but to succeed, and it gives me all the fuel I need to fight. Except I can't go back to who I was; I need to blend a new me with the old me. I'm on the verge of a renaissance, a rebirth opportunity to shape my own happiness.

Divorcing in a foreign country comes with a multitude of challenges. I decide to leave my ex without seeking financial support, despite having the option. In doing so, I try to minimize the risk of losing my son in a custody battle across continents, a thought that fills me with terror. Now, I need to make a living on my own in one of the most expensive places on earth. I feel the pressure to make my small business grow fast. I'm in a very dark spot, and I need to see the light.

My parents are always there to lend an ear and share the highs and lows with me. But thousands of miles away from loved ones, I feel like no one has my back over here, even more so after losing my local "support system" of expat friends freshly met in San Francisco. It's surprising how being single suddenly complicates most of my relationships. It's as if I now have a somewhat contagious "divorcee condition." Both wives and husbands maintain a safe distance and deprive me of the much-needed social interactions that help keep me sane. I feel let down and betrayed by people I thought were close friends here. I miss my American friends from San Diego. I'm trying to make sense of all the emotions I'm experiencing:

sadness, anger, anxiety, helplessness...the list is long. I'm now convinced I can no longer afford to trust anyone, and I must fight on my own.

And yet...in a surprising twist, I find out that a few silent backers I hadn't considered actually support me and try to boost my business. Like the CEO who sends me countless business referrals without my knowledge. Like the compassionate mom on a gray October morning at the school playground. She sees my vulnerability, listens to my worries, and reassures me, saying I'll figure it out. Two months later, her husband "miraculously" offers to collaborate on a major deal. It puts me back on my feet and helps me turn a corner for good. These incredible allies are silently rescuing me. They restore my faith in humanity and redefine friendship. My strength and hope for a bright future grow each day.

It's December 2014, and I'm getting ready for our very first Christmas as a split family. I want to create a festive home for my son with a delicious meal, lovely decorations, and new traditions. I also choose to mark this turning point in my life. Despite the messiness of divorce, freedom is a beautiful thing I should celebrate. I treat myself to a meaningful ornament: a stunning pair of angelic wings. They glisten with sparkling crystals—bright, white, and as delicate as a soft breeze. In what is now a yearly Christmas tradition, I silently unpack my beautiful white wings while my son is decorating the Christmas tree. I pause and smile, intense emotions resurfacing. I reflect on what I have accomplished and what I'm capable of. I hang the wings beside my father's bookcase, reminding me of my regained freedom and my hopes for a better future. Now, I can fly high and make the best of 2015 in the land of freedom and opportunities.

"If everything was always easy, life would be fucking boring."
—Frank

With the new year, I'm taking charge of my destiny. I'm on a mission to grow exponentially. The colossal self-help market booming in the US is turning me into an information junkie. I consume books, blogs, podcasts, gurus, conferences, and on TV, Oprah reminds me to feel empowered and live my best life. Now, it's about setting goals and pursuing them. The only limit is time, not imagination.

Add the Silicon Valley mindset, and I'm constantly improving. It's a real bubble where we all chase success. I stay ahead of trends, scale at lightning speed, and learn from the best leaders and innovators on the planet. There's no other ecosystem like this, and it's exhilarating. Here, the motto is "fail fast, fail often." They say an entrepreneur should fail eight times starting a company before succeeding. It's a major shift from the unforgiving French approach: We tend to shut down hope after the first failure. In Silicon Valley, there are no safe shores in sight. Possibilities are endless if you push yourself.

It's not for everyone, though. Stay comfortable in the familiar or choose growth—you can't have both. Like growing muscles, micro-tears are needed. Pain, adjustment, and discomfort fuel growth. Silicon Valley takes immense effort, so explorers come and go. Moving here challenges everything I knew, like that tolerance to failure, for instance. Openness to new perspectives is tiring, but I find it essential for true integration.

Fun fact: Immigrants represent over 45% of Silicon Valley's workforce, and 55% of America's billion-dollar startups have an immigrant founder. Despite this, the years-long immigration process is agonizing to me, facing rejections and fearing the loss of job-tied visas. Even with my efforts to integrate, pay taxes, and support US businesses, I am an outsider, an alien, a green card holder with limited rights. Experiencing these challenges has completely transformed my perspective on immigration, both in the US and in Europe. That doesn't deter my desire to be American, but I know firsthand the unfairness of this endless process, a complex issue to figure out.

It's January 6, 2016, and today, my son and I are both officially becoming American. This day feels very special for so many reasons. First, this country is now our true home, a place where we are accepted unconditionally. The ability to exercise my voting rights is also a monumental privilege. An official letter from President Obama congratulating us captures the essence of these milestones. It's also a symbol of the new era of hope and inclusion underway in this country. Our oath ceremony is a beautiful and memorable moment full of emotions. Unexpectedly, I also sense an immense and reassuring shield of protection enveloping us during the ceremony. Although the initial turbulence in my separation has diminished, I take great comfort in knowing that a judge would now make sure to keep my son on US soil in a custody battle. With this citizenship, a feeling of security hits me like a massive and powerful wave. I cry like a baby for hours, overwhelmed with relief. I'm on an emotional high! The weight is off my shoulders, and we are free to move on without any fear ever.

"There is nothing stronger than a broken woman who has rebuilt herself." —Hannah Gadsby

The journey is quite long, but I regain my initial strength and confidence, and then some.

My determination as a single mother makes me fierce at work, too. I work tirelessly, sacrificing sleep, to reach life goals one after another, and I'm having fun through it all. My business is soaring, building a strong reputation in B2B tech as a marketing fixer—a woman who gets results. I secure prestigious clients, change trajectories, and make many hires.

Multiple factors contribute to these outcomes. However, I firmly believe the deep self-understanding I went through plays a pivotal role in my accomplishments. Expatriation helps me define my professional value and position my business. I can now articulate it to prospects. I bring expertise along with a fresh outsider perspective. My direct, no-BS French communication style, sprinkled with a positive California attitude, is also what many CEOs find refreshing.

I proudly share my victories with my son: His trouper attitude, kindness, and stellar behavior have been instrumental in my upward trajectory. He's a true partner in this quest, and I'm so proud to show him the importance of self-belief and hard work. Step by step, I can figure things out. And I now realize how mistaken I was in thinking I had to face it all alone. My family, friends, and unexpected allies near me provide invaluable assistance. A network reboot introduced me to amazing individuals; they support, encourage, and help heal me, restoring trust. Even during the pandemic, my friend Christine selflessly cares for me after surgery. What a difference from my sad experience a few years back! This unfailing support deeply touches me.

"If you want to lift up humanity, empower women."
—Melinda Gates

Women often ask me how I manage to thrive in a very male-dominated tech world, and the answer is quite simple.

I see Silicon Valley as a tech-centric version of Hollywood. It's a world of many ambitious individuals striving for success. Then you have the powerful few and many deceivers who promise to fulfill their aspirations. I had to learn to navigate these complex relationships and quickly get away from toxic personalities. Women make up only 33% of the tech-related workforce. It's undeniable: It can be a paternalistic or sometimes sexist environment, limiting women's chances of promotion or equal pay. Moreover, men hold 91% of employee and founder equity in Silicon Valley. Despite this, I thrive with confidence, being fearless, defying gender roles, and seizing opportunities. I make a point to find allies and ask for what I want in a non-apologetic way. That's when my French direct communication style comes in handy. The most important career decisions are often made when we are not in the room. So, I make sure my worth is well known and have powerful allies advocating for me.

In my journey to build a strong network, I join organizations supporting women in all areas of life. I feel a strong sense of belonging and profound respect for them: They empower women, provide incredible opportunities, and foster lifelong friendships. These circles of sisters are something I hadn't experienced to this extent in France. These organizations enrich my life with valuable connections and moments of reflection.

And don't forget the men in tech! I love working with so many professionals who understand the importance of supporting women. They are actively breaking down the boys' club culture with grace and intelligence. Some miss the mark but can still learn. Like the creative director who refuses to hear me reject his campaign pitch three times, despite valid reasons. Not able to change my mind, he asks, "Why are you so mad? Don't you see it's a good idea?" There is a sad tendency to label decisive women as "aggressive" and praise men for leadership. I calmly explain that I'm not mad, just firm, as our limited resources will cause the campaign to fail. I ask if he would accuse a man of being mad for rejecting his pitch. He reflects, admits he wouldn't, and appears surprised at his own behavior. We move on, smiling. Obviously, it doesn't always end that well. I have my fair share of toxic men to deal with along the way, and I painfully learn not to let it deter me.

As I overcome obstacles and make my way to the top, I hope to inspire other women to rise up, bringing as many as I can by my side. I finally find my true calling in supporting women as a way to give back. That's the legacy I want to create. Alongside my consulting business, I teach marketing, advise entrepreneurs, and mentor professionals. It's a fantastic chance to support women and businesses. However, it feels like a small contribution with so many women struggling for freedom, financial independence, and success.

In 2020, I find an incredible opportunity with How Women Lead. It's a network of 20,000 American women leaders who serve on corporate boards and promote gender equity. I meet incredible women and soon become a volunteer, the marketing group co-lead, and a global advisor to foreign entrepreneurs advocating for reproductive health, rights, and justice.

A year later, I also become a limited partner at How Women Invest, the organization's private equity fund supporting female-founded startups. It's crucial because despite women launching 40% of US companies, only 2.4% of venture funding goes to them. You read that right...how can the US be so far behind? How can we disrupt the venture landscape in Silicon Valley? I'm determined to be part of the solution. As I join this fund, I can increase investments in female-founded companies. I can support innovative and impactful initiatives that wouldn't see the light of day. It's a full-circle change!

In June 2023, sixty-eight of us have the privilege of ringing the closing bell at NASDAQ, the world's second-largest stock exchange in NYC. Most Silicon Valley enthusiasts aspire to live this experience. I never thought I would get to live it myself, so it is a dream come true, especially on my forty-fourth birthday! We're shooting a ten-minute live show. It is broadcast on news TV internationally. Our goal? To empower ten thousand women to invest in women through the launch of The New Table campaign.

Before the show begins, we experience that "wow" moment of seeing our campaign featured on Times Square's seven-story tower. Picture sixty-eight overjoyed women, each trying to capture the perfect selfie! The anticipation fills the studio as we are finally let in. Just five minutes before we go live! I know my family and friends will be watching the ceremony on TV. The excitement has me grinning from ear to ear, cheering along with others. No need for a pre-show warmup! The countdown is over, and everything happens in a whirlwind: the inspiring speech from our fearless leader, Julie Castro Abrams, the bell ringing, the applause, the flood of congratulatory messages from everyone. The experience exceeds my expectations and leaves me on a high for hours. Our campaign kickoff is a win with hundreds immediately taking the pledge. I'm celebrating this major milestone for our cause with my fellow change-makers.

Somehow, this milestone feels like it is mine, too: an incredible step in my quest for growth and impact I never imagined reaching. It's hard to put into words the thrill of being part of this incredible moment. It would never have happened if I had stayed in France. California taught me to shoot for the stars, and this wild ride transformed me forever. Now, I'm a strong, happy, independent, and accomplished woman with a purpose bigger than myself.

I'm definitely living the American Dream, and I'm just getting started!

JULIE CANDELON

J ulie Candelon is a B2B marketing expert, business owner, and Silicon
Valley veteran. She is a fractional marketing executive, go-to-market
advisor, and mentor who empowers tech entrepreneurs and leaders to
accelerate revenue growth. Her unique perspective, data-driven marketing
approach, and result-focused leadership have earned Julie opportunities
to serve startups and Fortune 500 companies, including NVidia, Amazon,
RingCentral, Cumulus Networks, and EditShare. When she's not sailing
in the Bay Area or traveling the world with her son, Julie enjoys dancing,
photography, and exploring innovation, AI, or startup investing.

Website: www.jmarketing.team

LinkedIn: www.linkedin.com/in/jcandelon

Instagram: www.instagram.com/tipiwi/

Facebook: www.facebook.com/juliecandelon/

6

Texans Traveling

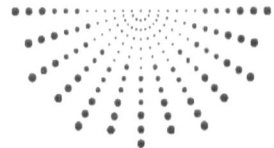

NATASHA ZIKE

H uddled in a dense crowd of strangers, pressed against the side of a
building under a small, flimsy awning, I hope to escape the freezing
rain of a winter storm in London. I am inadequately dressed—cold pint in
freezing hand, begging for its warming effects to kick in. I pause a moment
to relish the events that led to this.

Let me back it up. A lot. I'm a west Texas gal from a country town, and
while I traveled frequently as a kid, the methods of transportation and
destinations were very different. We were a low-income family living on
welfare. We tended to only travel when we needed to, and we often went to
places where people were like us in some way. I remember riding the packed
Greyhound bus with my mom to visit my grandparents or alone later as a
middle schooler to visit my boyfriend six hours away. Sometimes we would
hitchhike. When I was ten, my mom and I hitchhiked to a neighboring

town so we could play bingo. It was around this time I realized we probably shouldn't be doing this for safety's sake. Why was I the one to see this?

Around that time, my mom married a steady, salt-of-the-earth man who became a truck driver, and I had the joy of spending summers from elementary to middle school traveling cross-country with them. I saw most states east of Texas, up and down mountains, through forests, and in and out of truck stops. I remember Cherry Master slot machines and having to "hold it" 'til we got to the next truck stop! My CB radio handle was "Blue-Eyed Angel," and my mom's was "Something Special." She flirted with other truckers using her sexy pickup line, and many times she asked me to turn around in the cab, but I didn't know why, until one time, I snuck a glance to see her flashing another truck! If she were still alive, she'd be tickled that I added this crass moment that showcased her wild, free, and fun-loving spirit.

I road-tripped a lot as a kid, from summer youth camps and mission trips with church to riding in the back row of an old station wagon with my family. As I got older, I finally flew to distant lands such as New York City with my high school choir and again with my high school yearbook class right after 9/11. These trips were for specific reasons, like visiting family or singing at a cathedral, but they were not taken with the intent to expose myself to people and places unfamiliar to me or to photograph them and teach others about the new experiences I've had like my travel as an adult does. My early travels did, however, plant the seeds of curiosity in wanting to travel more and eventually move abroad.

When I got a job in high school, the first thing I saved my money to buy was a Canon Rebel X SLR camera so I could take "good photos." From a young age, I knew photography was a passion I wanted to pursue, and a couple of years after moving away for college, a co-worker asked me, "If you could be anywhere, doing anything, and money was no object, where would I find you?" I thought so hard about it I had to come back a few days later. "I just want to travel and take pictures," I finally said. A National Geographic photographer or movie maker was high at the top of my list. My interest in travel and photography led to the eventual creation of TexansTraveling, an online social presence and blog. TexansTraveling is where my husband and I enjoy sharing experiences in new places with our followers through photos, stories, and videos. I hope people experience new cultures they didn't expect, or that they feel the joy of the moment I'm capturing and find that they, too, want to travel and do the same.

Life lies more in the journey than in the destination—riding a Greyhound bus or hitchhiking with my mom as a kid; taking bus rides, a train, and many ski lifts to the top of the Schilthorn in Switzerland to see the Alps in every direction as far as the eye could see; laying down across the back row of an old station wagon on a road trip as a kid; riding a rib boat like a bucking bull over the choppy waves through Norwegian fjords; or sailing a smooth gondola ride in Venice, where your boyfriend proposes. Let's face it: We'll all have the same final destination, but what do we do with the in-between? For me, I want to soak up the earth and its experiences until it feels like the other side of it is next door.

Travel makes the world small and attainable while normalizing the lives, cultures, religions, and foods of others who live differently than you. Some of these you'll like, and some you won't, but either way, you'll hopefully gain an appreciation for the cultural differences in this world. It's so much bigger and grander than the small view where we started.

So, how did I end up in London, huddled under that freezing awning, and why did it keep happening day after day? Those strangers I mentioned were my new co-workers, and I had just moved to London for work with my husband (pre-kids). My husband had extensively road-tripped in the US, but until he met me, he had experienced limited international travel, and he certainly wouldn't have thought of moving abroad!

After working at Tableau Software for only three months, I boldly asked my new boss to move me to London as soon as possible. I had never even stepped foot in Europe, but I knew it was where I wanted to be. I figured if I was ever going to live abroad—a far-fetched stretch goal—I needed to seize the opportunity now to experience something completely new. My boss and her boss actually agreed, and so I made the jump in January 2015 with my husband and our three cats, who received their own pet passports!

Moving to London was far more difficult than I imagined! Even though I love learning new languages and practice them daily, I thought as long as I moved to an English-speaking country, it wouldn't be so hard. Living in another country has many more challenges than just understanding the language, it turns out! I had challenges knowing where to buy groceries or home furnishings, and when I located the store names and locations, I had to figure out how to bring things like a bed or groceries home on the Tube, in an Uber, or in a black cab.

We lived in two different Airbnbs during the first month while we searched for and then waited for our flat to become available. One was lovely on Hoxton Square in the hip Shoreditch district, and the other was in upper-class Kensington by Royal Albert Hall, but all the windows faced walls and made for a dimly lit flat. In the end, we moved into a once-in-a-lifetime flat immediately on the Thames in an area called Bermondsey. We were in

Cinnamon Wharf, a building that sometimes smelled of the spices it once held as a warehouse on the water, and we overlooked the most magnificent inlet. Half of the time, it just looked like mud, but as you sat and watched, the tide began to rise and fill this inlet, like lapping waves from an ocean on a beach, until it was full enough for a swim! Our sixth-floor flat overlooked it and the verdant houseboats full of lush greenery and stared directly out to Canary Wharf's financial district of densely packed skyscrapers. We were on the historic riverside street of Shad Thames (look it up!) and a block from Tower Bridge.

I had an incredible two-mile walk to work every day along the Thames, where thousands of years of history meshed with current-year urbanism. My office was the geographical hub for all of EMEA, a common business acronym for Europe, Middle East, and Africa. We had about 150 people in the office, maybe seventy-five of them were in sales like me, and we covered accounts all around EMEA, which were diverse in language, culture, and religion. Our sales reps and colleagues were just as diverse, and as you walked around the floor, you'd hear a different language on each row or even from desk to desk—English (in different dialects of British English, South African, Australian, American, New Zealander, and many more), Spanish (and many of its different dialects), Portuguese, Italian, Turkish, German, Swedish, Dutch, Russian, and more! My social media just this week reminded me of an event with some of my best girlfriends in London, each of us from a different country—Northern Ireland, Italy, France, the US, and Romania/Turkey.

Most of us were expats from other countries, and the few Londoners around welcomed us with open arms. We quickly made an eclectic friend group who worked together during the day and celebrated together at night, often en masse outside a pub, sometimes huddled under an awning if it was raining. This was London, though, where it often rains! Our French friends, among others, preferred to smoke cigarettes, and while I hated the smell, we all stayed outside together for those who needed their vice.

Every single night after work, almost the entire office, no matter the level, walked a block to the White Hart for a pint or five. My spouse would often join us, and I loved flitting from group to group like a butterfly tending my flowers. When the White Hart closed, a smaller group left to fill up on a "cheeky Nandos," a local chicken place that stayed open late. Every once in a while, we'd opt for The Refinery, which was this hip cocktail bar and cafe in our Blue Fin office building. I don't know if all businesses in London did this or just mine, but it was by far the most memorable tradition of my daily life in London—creating a community with my work colleagues from all around the world and learning about our differences.

My London work colleagues opened my mind to new experiences, cultures, food, and religions as well. Being from rural west Texas, I hadn't been exposed to any religions outside of Catholic and the Protestant flavors of Baptist, Southern Baptist, Methodist, and Church of Christ, and everyone I knew back then fit neatly into one of those categories. My hometown of Abilene, Texas, boasted of being in the Guinness Book of World Records for the Most Churches Per Capita, and often people would say it was the "Buckle on the Bible Belt." People didn't ask *if* you went to church but *where*, and sometimes *how often*.

Living in London was the polar opposite with its beautiful melting pot of people, and it was my first experience of having Muslim colleagues and friends. The Muslim colleague who sat across from me was married and English, and he had a full beard he said he didn't plan to cut because of his religion. The colleague next to me, Aytac (said "iTouch"), was Turkish and Muslim and was the most genial, warm person I met. He smoothed the transition to London culture for me, and I'm forever grateful. Another friend from Northern Ireland had been raised Christian, but after moving to Dubai, she had chosen to convert to Islam and marry. Before moving to London, she wore a hijab and traditional Muslim clothing, but she told me she struggled to find work while wearing it, even in the multiculturalism of London. As soon as she took it off for a new interview, revealing she was a strikingly beautiful blonde, she immediately received an offer for employment.

Because of her upbringing, she understood both Christian and Muslim ideologies, and she would regularly tell me how similar the religions are to one another, that Allah was love, and that the two religions preached similar beliefs but with different backgrounds. I thought that was surprising given the American media's coverage, and we engaged in lengthy discussions that I'm glad she was open to having. She is one of the many "soul-stirring" people who will forever shape me, along with the whole of this unique living experience abroad. It opened my mind even more to go past the mere acceptance of people's differences to find myself a champion and advocate for diversity, inclusion, and belonging in my daily work life.

A fellow American expat at my office with a travel blog told me her goals were to travel somewhere inside the UK every month and somewhere outside the UK every month. My husband and I took up that charge, and for the fourteen months we lived in London, we could do the same thanks to easily accessible travel and an intense curiosity for new experiences. In that time, we visited eighteen countries and over forty-five cities across three continents from Alaska to Turkey while working full time on a limited, single-income budget.

This list includes Ireland, Scotland, Wales, Amsterdam, Copenhagen, Rome (so many times that I actually considered myself "Romed-out" for a while!), Naples, Barcelona, Granada, Istanbul, a cruise from Vancouver to Anchorage, and another cruise through the Mediterranean from Rome, through Greece (and Santorini!), ending in Istanbul. We visited Seattle, many cities in Switzerland, Paris, Brussels and Brugge, Germany, Cambridge, the Lake District, and many, many more across Europe.

So I had my "trip" to London to live and then all these wonderful trips along the way to other places! Travel costs were cheap! We could fly to Dublin for £15 return each (round-trip) and stay in a hostel for not much more (though we opted for a private room). Spontaneity and good vibes ruled the itinerary. We would often pick the destination within a day or two of leaving, and I remember one time we were thinking of going to Copenhagen for the weekend when a friend invited us to Barcelona with him instead. It sounds wild, but when travel is that accessible, the world is your oyster!

One memorable trip was with a colleague from Canada and my husband. The three of us decided to see what Amsterdam's King's Day was like. King's Day is the official celebration of the birthday of the King, Willem-Alexander, and their family's last name is Oranje-Nassau. Can you guess what color the entire city turns on King's Day? One guess. A flight would have been cheap and easy, but with the suggestion to show up two hours before the flight, it was faster to take the train. Better yet, we packed a picnic, complete with wine, and had a mini celebration on the way there—something we wouldn't have been able to do on a plane.

We were decked out in our brightest orange feather boas, hats, sunglasses, shirts, and anything orange we could find, and we made it into the city center, where we were greeted with lovely, loud, and joyful crowds. We were in Amsterdam! Who wasn't having a good time? We quickly found our way to one of many bridges where a parade of boats passed underneath along the canals—decked out in orange, of course, and filled with orange-clad party-goers, blasting "Uptown Funk" and other feel-good tunes. We watched this floating parade for a long while, and eventually, we made our way to a large music venue with a massive stage for electronic music. We didn't know what we were doing. We didn't have a plan. We just showed up and let the city guide us, and it was one of the best experiences I've ever had.

The next morning was the Dutch flower parade that slowly snakes its way twenty-six miles from the sea, through flower fields near Lisse to the historic city of Haarlem. Each vehicle is decorated to the brim with spring flowers of tulips, daffodils, and hyacinths, and the smell was pungent and sweet. We watched from Lisse, near its city center, and enjoyed the beautiful floats in this annual tradition that's occurred for over seventy years! It started back in 1947 to celebrate the end of World War II and to help people socialize. By the early 1950s, the event already had over five hundred thousand visitors annually from around the world, and now it's over one million each year.

After the parade concluded, we walked ten minutes to the famous Keukenhof Gardens, one of the world's largest flower gardens, boasting over seven million flower bulbs each year! If you choose to go, I highly recommend buying your tickets in advance, as early as October the year before, as this garden is only open for eight weeks each year from mid-March to mid-May, and it welcomes around 1.5 million people each year, or twenty-six thousand people a day! The day of the parade is their busiest day of the year.

However, as I mentioned, we hadn't actually planned out this trip ahead of time, so did we know this? No! Were we lucky? I'm happy to report, yes! We bought tickets and entered this sweeping landscape of floral beauty. Tulips, hyacinths, daffodils, and more types of each flower than we knew existed—there were 800 types of tulips there alone!—spanned in front of us in all directions, covering almost eighty acres. It was a photographer's paradise! The beauty here is that we didn't have other plans we needed to run off to—we were able to fully appreciate each moment and stop every few feet for photos. There were three of us, so my husband and I also had a photographer to take our picture. The opportunities were endless, and a favorite is one where we sat together in a large wooden clog with a giant Dutch windmill behind us!

We noticed that we hadn't seen people in a while, and it was already late afternoon. We kept walking about, enjoying the gardens, until we finally realized the park had closed *hours* before, and we had been wandering around taking photos after closing. We saw many workers who never questioned us or shooed us on our way, and we left soon after, having experienced one of the best days of relaxed beauty, nature, and bliss we could have imagined.

These were no longer the trips of my youth. These experiences, including the ones I have now, allow me to take in culture and nature and history, and I often stop every few feet for photos to savor the view, the smells, or the feel of the wind. My friends understand, and even if they grumble, they let me indulge in my passion.

With so many beautiful and interesting locations I've visited, it's hard to decide which few make it into this book and why. I'll finish by sharing the end of a three-week European holiday enjoyed with visiting friends starting in London, through Paris, to many cities and islands in southern Italy (Rome, again??) and Greece, ending in Istanbul.

On our way to Turkey, we passed through the Dardanelles Strait, which at the time was under a tenuous conflict that made us doubt if we would make it to Istanbul. Thankfully, all was well, and we found our way to the city that straddles the continents, with one foot in Europe and the other in Asia. Five times a day, over loudspeakers from the minarets, we heard the stirring Muslim call to prayer known as the ezan. We visited the large, well-known Blue Mosque, built in 1616. The dress code here includes long pants (covered knees), covered shoulders, no shoes, and women must cover their heads. If ladies don't have a head covering, they'll provide one, and thankfully, being European and all by then, I had a fashionable, light scarf with me to repurpose for my head, and so did my friend. We took in the architectural brilliance and craftsmanship of the structure, and thankfully for me, we could also take photos from the inside while still remaining respectful.

Directly across from the Blue Mosque is a building of equal brilliance, but with a unique history, called the Hagia Sophia (said ay-yah so-fee-uh), a UNESCO World Heritage Site. In its history, it has been an Orthodox church, a Roman Catholic cathedral, a mosque, a museum, and then a mosque again in 2020. Due to its varied religious past, its keepers respected the history and kept paintings of Mary and Jesus up, even though they're not a part of Islam.

After visiting these sites, we took a small boat tour to the Asian side of the bay to finally step foot in Asia. We didn't stay long, and when it was done, we crossed the water again to shop at the Grand Bazaar in Istanbul. What a busy place with smells of spices filling the air! Its size was massive, with sixty-one covered streets and over four thousand shops! Wikipedia says that it attracts up to four hundred thousand visitors *daily* and was listed as "number one among the world's most-visited tourist attractions and is regarded as one of the first shopping malls in the world." I haggled for a colorful Turkish lantern, my friend bought it in a chandelier form, and we both enjoyed discounted luxury scarves and bags.

Beyond the history, the food was a true highlight of Turkey, including Turkish delight, kebabs, and testis. The testi kebab is cooked in a pottery jug filled with meats such as lamb, beef, or chicken and veggies such as carrots, celery, onions, garlic, and potatoes. It reminds me somewhat of a southern stew. They have hot clay pots filled with this kebab mixture over a bright fire. When it was time to eat, they cracked the bottom of the single-use pot open as part of an elaborate, flamboyant show and poured its delicious contents onto my plate. Döner kebabs had already easily become my favorite food in London, besides meat pies, and this testi kebab took the cake. It was so juicy and flavorful. With the goal of experiencing moments like a local, we enjoyed dinner with a traditional nargile outside under the stars.

I'll share a hilarious part of the trip that we still laugh about year after year as the video pops up in our memories online. Europe, along with other places in the world, use bidets to clean their tushies in the bathroom (water closet, loo, lavatory, john, toilet, etc.). There are many variations of this, and most I've seen offer a toilet across the room from a bidet-only feature that you sit on (or do you hover? Who do you ask?). The hotel where we stayed offered a toilet with a bidet in it, and while that's not the funny part, my friends showed us their bidet while I was filming. (Why? Because by this point in the story, you should know that's how I am.) The water pressure from the bidet without someone on it shot like a rocket onto the shower wall *across* the room! All I could think and say was, "Who needs that much pressure?!" A funny moment, memorialized forever on film.

On the last morning, we ventured out early in the morning for one final experience. In a Turkish bath, people are mostly naked, and there's not a single part of you that won't get wet as lots of suds are involved. The room is much like a sauna. You'll sweat on your own, and your pores will love you for it, especially after a multi-week journey. Men and women are in separate baths. There were times it was really nice, and other times it was surreal. This bath house has existed here since 1584, and the locker key they give you reminds you of this while you lay in the steamy silence: "1584 Hamamı." The paint is chipped off in many areas of the wall, and the room is filled with a large, warm, marble centerpiece platform on which you lay. Everything is damp. Eyeglasses were a poor choice for this girl who got ready too quickly that morning. They fog instantly. Don't slip on the marble. I'm guided to lie down and relax.

During this time, I notice more of the architecture, the date on the key-chain, trying to remember how to say the name of the place that has the different C and different S in it. Seeing the beauty of the place and not being able to capture it in film, I start counting shapes to cement the details as I lie alone in silence. Worker number fifty-two returns and pours warm water all over me, scrubbing with a loofah glove and sudsy craziness. I think she sadistically gets pleasure from making it fall in your face, as she reinforced later while washing my hair and rubbing soapy hands in my eyes. She never told me when she would pour water on my face, which I didn't like, but it was all a part of the experience, with as much leisure time in the bath as I wanted. Somehow, it only lasted forty-five minutes.

The stories that resonate with me recall beautiful views, steep climbs, and connections. They're the stories where I learned something or created lasting memories, and they're intensified when I'm able to share them with others through photography or film. Travel unites us, makes borders smaller, and makes the unique more attainable. The friends and colleagues I met in London were from so many parts of the world, yet we created rich friendships and a community despite our differences. We huddled under awnings in the freezing rain together and enjoyed many travels around the city, country, continent, and world together.

Travel has made me a better citizen of the world, appreciating different foods, cultures, religions, and people. I started as a small-town, west Texas girl with little exposure to the world, by no fault of my own, and I'm proud of the growth I've done as a human and citizen of this rich and vibrant world we live in. Travel has made me a champion of helping others, of all walks of life, find their own place in the world, and I find joy in doing the work to make experiences better for all people so we can all live richer and fuller lives, with the little time we are each given. Life is short, so enjoy the hell out of it! I strive to soak it all up as quickly as I can, imparting the hard-won wisdom I've learned upon listening ears at any chance I get. I hope you'll continue our journey together from here by following the photos and videos I share on TexansTraveling as I continue to travel the world. Ciao!

NATASHA ZIKE

N atasha is a best-selling author, passionate global leader, speaker, and nonprofit advisor, whose whole-person, inclusive approach to business creates environments where individuals thrive and business succeeds. She has spent the last nineteen years in the corporate technology space in the US and London and is a global leader at a Fortune 50 software company. Her empowering messages guide others to live purposefully and joyfully in the face of adversity, making the most of this short life, no matter where we started. She is passionate about diversity, equity, inclusion, and belonging (DEIB) and works to create safe spaces for employees to feel empowered to bring their full, authentic selves to work.

She resides in Austin, Texas, with her husband and two active young children.

LinkedIn: www.linkedin.com/in/natashazike/

Instagram: www.instagram.com/natashazike/

7

Love Stinks

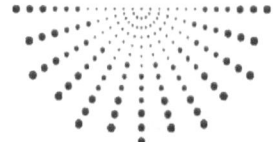

DEBRA BLUE

In 2009, after a divorce, I found and updated a list of lifetime goals and dreams that I started as an assignment in my 9th grade history class in the 80s. The list was updated to include all seven continents and roughly fifty countries. That year alone, I visited Singapore, Bali, Yogyakarta, Hong Kong, and Kuala Lumpur. This was the year I also made a commitment to myself to visit one new country per year and eventually set foot on every continent.

Four years later, I found myself in a new relationship with a man named Ed. I was hoping that this time I had broken my habit of dating "the bad boy" and found someone who was more similar to me—liberal, gainfully employed, had insurance, thought about saving for retirement, and liked traveling—all typical adult things in my opinion. Not wanting to waste time, I began asking him to travel with me to see if we were compatible.

I wanted to see if he could put himself into uncomfortable situations, somewhere where he may not speak the language or where he might need to ask for help. There were out-of-town trips at first, then out-of-state, and finally, I asked him to go on one of my huge bucket list trips.

Along with thousands of other people, I have always been fascinated with Mount Everest and the people that climb it. I knew I would never be a climber, but there was a huge pull to see the base camp where the climbers start their journeys and to see the amazing Sherpas who live year-round in the region. My journey would be hiking to 17,598 feet over multiple days to Everest Base Camp (EBC) and celebrating my birthday along the trek.

When I asked Ed if he wanted to join me, there was some hesitation, but he did say yes. I booked the trip, and we started walking...a lot. A few months into training, he was having issues where his legs would seize up when we walked. After finding the right doctor, Ed was diagnosed with exertional compartment syndrome and required surgery on both legs, with an estimated twelve-month recovery.

We scheduled surgery, and I moved the trip out a year. Weeks later, on April 25, 2015, Nepal suffered a 7.8 magnitude earthquake that shattered the country. It hit days before our original flight was scheduled to leave.

After a year of healing, for both Ed and Nepal, we landed in Kathmandu. The people were still struggling, and the infrastructure was still in disrepair. Many buildings were in piles where they had collapsed, and people were sleeping in tents on vacant lots. Despite the difficult circumstances, everywhere we went, the spirit of survival and hope was alive and well. As we walked around, exploring the city and getting amped up for the big trek, everyone we met was kind and grateful for the tourism that was bringing money back into the country.

April 27, 2016

Finally, the day came to fly to Lukla Airport, also known as Tenzing-Hillary Airport, or one of the most dangerous airports in the world due to the multiple risks associated with taking off and landing. The airport is on a mountainside and sits at a fairly high elevation, with intermittent weather, plus an incredibly short runway. While I white-knuckled anything I could grab onto during our landing, Ed assured me that we would be fine.

When I departed the twin-prop plane, I could not believe that I was finally there. I was going to hike in the Himalayas, the "abode of the snow" in Sanskrit. I was at the home of the highest peaks in the world. Usually, I'm good at hiding my emotions, but I could not hold back the tears at the realization that I was finally here. The air felt cool on my skin and did not have a scent that I could label, other than fresh.

The hike to Phakding was beautiful. The trail follows a river almost the entire way. It was our introduction to the sheer beauty of the region, seeing the amazing people who live and work here, a variety of animals, and the various trail conditions. We came across stupas (dome-shaped Buddhist shrines), a slew of brightly painted prayer rocks in green, blue, red, yellow, and white, plus the beginning of similarly colored strings of prayer flags that dominate the trails.

After putting our bags down, we went to order our first dinner of the journey. I ordered vegetable curry, and Ed ordered chicken curry. That took me aback, but I decided to bite my tongue instead of blurting out, "What the f-ck are you doing?" One day prior, we had attended a briefing session about the hike. This is where the guides take time to meet hikers in their groups and cover ground rules. With the Sagarmatha National Park area being primarily Buddhist, animals are not killed in the region. Also, refrigeration does not exist, so if you order meat, there's no telling when it was carried up into the mountains, and it is probably not very fresh.

About four hours later, the grumbling, gurgling, and bubbling were in full force in my Ed's intestines. Soon after, the first of many explosions happened. It continued all night and into the morning. I gave him Imodium and an antibiotic. In my travel journal, I would write, "I am his number one fan, and I can't make it stop." I went to bed hoping it would calm down overnight, only to be woken up every hour by the joyous symphony of food poisoning. This forced the development of a comfort level that I never thought I could have with another person.

April 28, 2016

I had to tell our guide that there was no way Ed could make the day's hike, but due to being on a schedule, we were asked to try.

We walked a short way from the hotel, across one of the many suspension bridges in the area, and he felt the urge again. He begged our guide to find a bathroom before he had an accident. There was a single building with a squatty potty (i.e., hole in the ground), and in he went. Twenty minutes later, when he emerged, I could not tell if he was laughing or crying, but I could see sweat beading down his face. He said he absolutely could not hike that day, so we went back to the hotel while our guide changed our itinerary. Safely back in our room, Ed would tell me, "I decorated the wall of that bathroom with confetti. It was a terrible experience, and I am so sorry this is happening." I asked, "Why did you decide to eat the chicken when we were told yesterday to eat vegetarian while we were up here?" He looked at me dumbfounded and said, "I did not even hear them say that."

April 29, 2016

The following morning, as we packed for the day's hike, Ed handed me a sunshirt that he had borrowed the previous day. As soon as I noticed a brown stain on the sleeve, I handed it back to him and said, "I am going to let you keep this as a souvenir." When we walked outside, we saw a small horse saddled up and ready to go. It would be his taxi for the climb ahead of us. Neither of us being too keen on horses, it was not how either of us would have wanted the trip to go, but he needed more rest, and we needed time to acclimate.

The hike took me a couple of hours longer than his ride. It was a significant climb, and we had lost a day to acclimate. We were originally set to spend two nights in Namche Bazaar, but now, it would only be one. The town was a magical place for me. The way the buildings curve around and dip between the hills is reminiscent of rice terraces. There are hotels of every variety, small shops with necessities and trinkets, and I even found a cafe with really good espresso.

During the day's hike, I had pushed through my fear of heights, crossing five suspension bridges, with the last one almost buckling my knees. Occasionally, I would look up from the trail to enjoy the scenery and the huge mountains surrounding me and take the deepest breath of fresh mountain air that is possible for someone with acute asthma. On the trail, there were donkeys carrying loads of supplies, tethered together with at least ten in each group, as well as porters with two to three times their body weight strapped to their backs. As hardworking as they are, they always said "namaste" when passing other people.

Ed and I started having nightly chats about how our day was, what we saw, what was our favorite thing, and what was challenging. His biggest memory of the day was "feeling like the horse did not want me on its back and thinking it was going to buck me off on a cliffside" or "feeling like I was going to pass out when I had to cross the suspension bridges, due to my low energy." I would share that I got scared on the suspension bridges and would check to see if any animals were beginning to cross from the opposite side; if so, I would just wait for them to get across. There was one point when I was walking across the highest one, and two people had stopped to take photos, and in my moment of panic, I said, "You have to move because I am about to freak the fuck out if I do not make it across quickly."

As I went to show him the photos I had taken, I realized that the card in my camera was not fitting snugly, and it had saved only a fraction of the photos I had taken over the last seven hours! Luckily, I was able to fix it with a small, folded piece of paper.

That night, before dinner, our guide explained that if Ed could not hike the following day, I would need to make the decision to leave him there and continue to EBC without him. Luckily, he was better by morning. The thought of doing this journey without him just felt wrong and not as fun.

April 31, 2016

The day started rough. I wrote, "What a birthday, quite possibly the best and worst rolled into one." I now also had dysentery; my heart was pounding, my lungs felt weak, and every step made me feel nauseous. Despite it all, we took off for Tengboche.

The trail took us deeper into the Himalayas, with drop-offs along the way and our first sighting of yaks. Luckily, they wear bells so you can hear them coming and move to the inside of the trail. They apparently have been known to accidentally push people off the cliff edge. We called the hike that day my "zombie walk." It was incredibly slow and required multiple breaks and the use of hiking poles. Every step felt like I was walking through mud. I just wanted to cry and lie down. A group of elderly women on the trail asked, "Are you ok? Do you need anything?" I was so upset that I felt ill, that I had missed a day to acclimate, but still so overjoyed to just be there.

Once we came upon the village, we were greeted by the Tengboche Monastery and multiple prayer wheels. We took the time to spin each wheel leading into the town. From there, we could finally see the peak of Everest, or Sagarmāthā, in the background amongst the many other mountains. It was surreal to finally see it.

At dinner, to my surprise, the staff began singing Happy Birthday, and multiple cakes were brought out. It was my forty-third birthday, and another guest was turning fifty. I was grateful to be here and happy that I was with a partner who was calm and saw the beauty in everything, even with our challenges. Everyone we encountered so far was so incredibly kind and sincere, especially our guide and porter.

We would go to bed early that night, too tired for our usual check-in.

May 1, 2016

The following day's hike was easier. I remember the beauty and scent of pink rhododendrons blooming everywhere along the beginning of the trail that passed a nunnery. Finally, hiking above the tree line, we walked into territory that looked like something out of a science fiction movie. We would both joke that "scenes from Star Wars could have been filmed here." The valleys were tan with the smallest dark green shrubs, surrounded by brown and gray rocky cliffs; layered behind those were snow-covered peaks.

We made it to Dingboche. The village is nestled in a canyon, and one of the first things you notice when you hike in is a large white stupa and baby yaks grazing on the hills. We sat down for a few minutes and snapped photos, then heard a very common noise in the area: a helicopter. We had seen them a couple of times most days and knew they typically were used for emergency evacuations. I looked at Ed and said, "Please tell me that that does not look like a rescue basket with a body bag underneath that helicopter." He sadly did not disagree with me, so we hoped we were confused about what we saw and took off for that night's hotel.

Our room was the last one where we would have our own ensuite bathroom. Unfortunately, a raw sewage aroma was included with the room due to the ensuite. The main area of the hotel, where people congregate to talk, play games, and eat, was heated by a wood-burning stove that was fueled by yak dung. In my journal, I wrote, "We have arrived at the shit hotel." Despite the smell, yak dung does make great fuel, and the primary area was warm and cozy.

After dinner, we laughed together as we did our ritual body wipe-style cleaning. All modesty had been thrown out the window, and we were comfortable with doing this task in front of one another, as well as admitting to the sheer stench of our bodies. It was probably good that we each had our own sleeping bag, and neither of us wanted to have sex at this point of the hike.

We had already been capturing classy photos of our body wipe bathing experiences, but Ed took things to a whole new level while we were here. The bathroom at this place had a door, but unfortunately, that door also had a window, and the toilet was missing its seat. I went in to use the facilities and heard a cackling laugh that I now call the "crazy old mountain man laugh." Ed was capturing a video of me trying to hover but failing and having to brace myself using my arm on the wall behind me.

That night, it snowed. The combination of altitude, coldness, and dryness from the snow made the air feel thin. Even with our setbacks, and the jokes we were making, I felt like I was in a dream.

May 2, 2016

I barely slept due to increasing pressure and white noise inside my head. I felt horrible and did not want to push myself and possibly trigger a headache. I stayed at the hotel and let Ed go on the acclimatization hike to a ridge above the village. I watched a toddler play for what seemed like hours, first with a bucket of water and a cup, then watched them stack up rocks. The whole time, I was able to see the trail that Ed was on and wished I was there with him. At some point that afternoon, I felt the tell-tale tingle of an oncoming cold sore. Just what I needed.

When Ed got back, I felt even worse. I asked him to lie down with me and just hold onto me while we took a nap. For a brief moment, I felt safe and felt like things would be ok.

At dinner, our guide, once again, began discussing options with us. I could pay for a helicopter to come and get me and take me back down to Kathmandu, and Ed could go to EBC, or I could keep pushing forward and risk getting really sick, requiring a helicopter ride, which I would rather avoid. The option we proposed was to completely change our itinerary and hike back down into the tree line. I felt like I was giving up on a dream, but I had read enough about altitude sickness and how it can quickly change, so I knew it was my best option for staying up in the mountains. I honestly thought Ed would take me up on my offer to have him see EBC without me.

That night, I thought I would be cute. I was feeling mixed emotions. On the one hand, I felt very vulnerable due to being sick, but on the other hand, I felt incredibly supported and comforted by Ed. I pulled him into our hotel room, dropped to my knee, and asked, "Will you be my committed life partner?" He turned as white as a sheet, and I had to explain that I did not say marriage, or legal, just committed. Needless to say, he did not find it as romantic or amusing as I did, but it did allow us to have a very honest conversation about how we wanted the rest of the trip to be. He said that it was my bucket list to see EBC, not his, and that he wanted us to stay together because that's the point of traveling together, sharing the experience.

We were so thankful that it was just the two of us, a guide and a porter, or there would not have been an option to turn around and hike at a lower altitude, completing our time up in the mountains.

May 3, 2016

As everyone else from the guest house took off on the trail, we hiked back from where we had been the previous day. It was heartbreaking to watch people head towards EBC, but as soon as we got back into the tree line, I could feel my body being relieved of some of the pressure. My headache was still there but started to subside, and my breathing was getting easier. I was so happy I actually hugged a tree.

Once we got back to the monastery, there was time to relax and hike around the small village. It was there that Ed and I left some of the ashes of my friend's grandmother in the majestic Himalayas, overlooking the monastery on one side and a drop-off on the other, with the ever-present prayer flags whipping in the cold wind. We sat down and watched thick gray clouds roll in and talked about both wanting to be cremated, not buried. I shared that "I want to have someone scatter my ashes all over the world, in my favorite places."

May 4, 2016

The hike back down to Namche Bazaar also felt good. We were both incredibly happy to be able to take a shower again, with warm water even, and overjoyed that I was feeling a little better. I took an adorable photo of Ed taking a nap when I came back into the room after my shower. He was wrapped like a burrito in the cutest flowery blanket, wearing his trademark knit red hat. It would later dawn on me that I was dating someone that looked like the traveling gnome.

The dinner hall was full that night. At a nearby table was a group of Russian climbers. They were talking about how it was too late for a summit bid on Everest, so they were going to pick another peak in the area. One was missing the tip of his nose and the tips of many of his fingers. Even with the adversity that he once faced, he was still obviously in love with mountaineering. Most people would not understand that, but it made perfect sense to us.

As we prepared for bed, Ed said, "What do you want to do tomorrow?" "I want to take our time and explore the town, drink some good coffee, and just enjoy being here," I replied.

May 5, 2016

We spent the day sightseeing. We went to the Sherpa Culture Museum and spent time sitting in a café, talking about our experience so far. I would write, "many people never get to see this, and others don't want to…I can't imagine being content in one tiny corner of the world." We both like seeing the world, meeting people from other places, and trying to learn about their culture. It was comforting knowing that we were so aligned on that way of thinking and experiencing things.

One thing we did bring home from Namche Bazaar is a wooden, carved, white bear mask that now hangs in our living room.

That evening, we talked about the volume of plastic bottles we both used and came across on the trail. We had been using our own water bottles and purifying tabs until we both had gastrointestinal issues. At that point, our guide said we would be better off using bottled water. I am sure we are not the first people to hike in this area and wonder what can be done to preserve it and not destroy the environment with trash and pollutants.

May 6, 2016

We made the hike back down the hardest switchbacks and multiple suspension bridges to Phakding. The nice thing is that we felt like we had more time to enjoy the view and take more photos. It was probably because we were on our descent and could breathe better. We took photos of curly-haired horses, hotels we thought would be nice to stay in if we ever made it back, and carved stone prayer tablets. The sweetest thing we saw was a dog and baby cow hanging out in a yard together, the dog desperately trying to get the baby cow to play. It reminded me of us and how we tease one another to get the other person riled up.

It started to rain as we got closer to our accommodation for the night. I spent the stormy evening in the common area, updating my journal with the types of toilets we used along the way, what we had been eating, and stories of different people we met. Ed spent his time in our room, relaxing and going through his photos. When I got back into the room, Ed was cackling like a crazy old mountain man. "I took a great photo of you today. Do you want to see it?" He took it on the trail between Tengboche and Namche Bazaar. I had used one of the porters' bathrooms, which was a wooden platform with plywood walls and a hole cut into the bottom that dropped everything down a steep hill that it was built over. In the photo, I am running out with a horrible look on my face because bees were swarming up from the hole.

May 7, 2016

Round two in Lukla greeted us with inoperable showers and another joyous toilet experience. My entry reads, "One toilet for twenty people that has had the same turd stuck in the bottom of it for who knows how long... every time you flush, it washes away a minuscule amount of it, like a river that slowly smooths out a rock's surface."

There we were, taking wet wash baths and marveling at the idea that we had just hiked for eleven days in the Himalayas. We had pushed ourselves mentally and physically and seen the most beautiful mountains in the world, but we were ready to go home and plan another trip here after showering and using a private toilet.

That evening, we were looking forward to being able to use the internet at the hotel to check in with family and read the news, but rolling blackouts would make that impossible. On top of it, most of the other people in our hotel were getting drunk to celebrate the end of their hikes to EBC. My journal entry reads, "Stuck here with loud twenty-something-year-olds, having no clean clothes, and body funk that just won't go away." I was also envious that they were celebrating a completed journey, where I felt I had failed.

May 8, 2016

Our porter found us at breakfast and came to say goodbye. We wish we could help him with English lessons so he would have other work opportunities. He greeted us with a smile every day, and every day, we carried a little more of our own gear. We understood how physically demanding his job was and wanted to make sure we were doing our part.

After packing, we went to the airport. Unfortunately, it was a cloudy day, and only a handful of flights got out. We would have to stay another night. That evening, we ended up talking to a brother and sister from Australia who were also stuck for an additional night. We made a pact to get a helicopter out if we ended up being there for too many days.

I was no longer amused with anything, I was having a hard time seeing the beauty surrounding me, I did not feel like talking, and my cold sore needed its own zip code.

May 9, 2016

The clouds were rolling in and out all morning. I tried to stay patient and breathe the fresh air, soaking in the last of the views, but I kept crying because I was ready to fly out, and Ed was irritable, explaining, "I am tired of eating toast for breakfast, I just want some scrambled eggs." Luckily, by ten-thirty that morning, we were on our plane. Once we were back in Kathmandu, we said farewell to our guide. He had been the person in charge of our trip, leading us from village to village, changing plans every time something happened, and ensuring we were enjoying our adventure.

That night and the following day, we strolled around close to the hotel in Kathmandu. We ran into people we had met on the trek, ate chicken curry, and laughed at all the obstacles we went through on the hike.

Ed would say that his favorite thing "was being there and experiencing it with you." For me, it was how small and insignificant I felt, being surrounded by giant mountains. I felt like a grain of sand, just a blip in time, but it was comforting. My most challenging part of the trip was not starting my altitude medication on day one due to poor advice. I could have potentially prevented myself from falling ill and gotten us both to EBC. Ed's biggest challenge was getting food poisoning and feeling like he let me down and delaying our progress.

There will always be trips where unexpected things happen: sickness, bathroom catastrophes, broken cameras, unexpected horsey rides. The ability to persevere, stay together, and try to be positive are key. I was with someone who had the ability to do all of that. Someone that I supported and that supported me when it was really needed.

Years Later

Fast forward to 2019. Ed and I went hiking at Enchanted Rock in Texas on New Year's Day. He stopped to grab water out of his backpack, and just as I was about to ask what was taking so long, I realized that he was down on one knee, holding a ring box. Ed then asked me to marry him, and I replied, "Are you sure?" In 2020, Ed and I eloped and took off for Argentina, where we would board a ship headed to Antarctica. We barely finished that trip, and the world came to a stand-still due to Covid. Like most people, we paused traveling to keep ourselves and others safe, but we will pick up the list soon and try to plan our final continent. I am also happy to share that our other trips have not included as many bathroom fiascos.

DEBRA BLUE

B orn into a military family, Debra was on the move from day one and learned how thrilling it can be to go to new places and learn about different people. This was the catalyst for her pursuing a cultural anthropology degree. After a short stint in NYC, Debra began a career in the tech industry that has spanned twenty-four years and has allowed her to revel in her travel addiction. Always seeking to continue learning, she obtained her MBA in 2018.

Debra and her husband have currently visited all but one continent and plan to continue their exploration of the world together.

LinkedIn: www.linkedin.com/in/debrablue/

Instagram: www.instagram.com/woman.spread/

8

Barrio Girl to City Lady

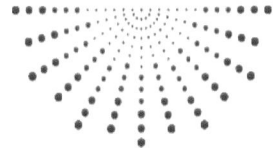

JANENE NIBLOCK

S tepping out into the Sydney Airport international arrivals terminal, I spotted two adorable boys, Liam and Oscar. *Holy smokes, these beautiful kiddos are going to be my stepsons!* Simon stood behind them smiling and quickly made his way over to hug me tightly and grab my luggage. Beaming at each other, we couldn't believe this was finally happening. We were moving in together, and I had traveled across the globe from Austin, Texas, to Sydney, Australia, to begin this new chapter in my life.

As we made our way up the stairs to the third floor of the apartment building (no elevator!), I spotted the 'Welcome Home' sign on the door that the boys had drawn. They were five and seven years old. We made our way in, and I took a deep breath, exhausted from the long journey. It was a super cute two-bedroom, one-bath apartment in a suburb called Hurstville. The boys had their own room when they stayed with us and of course, we now had our own room, too. The walls were a light soothing and calming blue. We had a small balcony where we could spot the train station just across the way. This picture-perfect space marked an important moment for us and was one I couldn't have imagined just eighteen months earlier.

Eighteen months prior, I was engaged...to someone else. I had organized a work dinner with the global sales and marketing team that had traveled to Austin for a company event. Sitting across the table from me was Simon, one of our sales reps from the Sydney office. We had a non-stop conversation that evening, and I complained to him about my current engagement. I whined about not being able to choose the wedding date I wanted, May 28, because my future step-monster-in-law wouldn't allow it. One of her granddaughters was graduating from high school that day, so *I* had to change the date to June 4 (keep this date in mind). Simon talked about his kids, so I figured he was definitely taken. He was adorable, and the way we carried on chatting over dinner, it was like the rest of the table wasn't even there. When the evening came to a conclusion, we went our separate ways.

Having doubts about getting married, I had been seeing a therapist to work through my worries about marrying into a family that didn't feel like a good fit. They were a rich family from Dallas. The first time they met my parents, they didn't gel at all. I had sad visions of celebrating holidays apart. I was a barrio girl from Laredo and didn't fit into their posh world. I had voiced my concerns to my fiance just in case he was having doubts too, but he wasn't, so I felt compelled to carry on with the plans. Deep down, though, something just didn't feel right. Since Simon and I both worked on the sales and marketing team, we still were in touch. Mostly about work stuff, but every now and then, the conversation over Yahoo chat (remember that tool?!) would turn a little more personal. He asked how things were going with the impending marriage, and I confided in him that

I was still apprehensive about moving forward. He visited again in April, and it had only been four months since our dinner connection. This time, I realized there was definitely some chemistry between us. Things were down to the wire with the wedding only eight weeks away, and I decided that even if I didn't end up having a relationship with Simon specifically, I still shouldn't be getting married because clearly my fiance wasn't the 'ONE.' I called off the wedding.

My family and friends were supportive of my choice, and I was so relieved. It's funny when things aren't meant to be; they are easy to unwind. All the plans and preparations were canceled. We had planned an intimate wedding in Laredo, Texas, in my aunt's beautiful backyard with a swimming pool and fuschia bougainvilleas in full bloom. So it wasn't like we lost a deposit or had to contact multiple vendors. The word quickly spread through the family trees, and I came out unscathed. But we did have a honeymoon credit! So, guess what happened next...

I booked a trip to visit Simon. August rolled around, and I headed to Sydney, Australia, to spend eight nights with Simon. It was magic. Looking back—who goes to Australia for eight days?! That was the first insight I had into how the world outside of the US lived, taking more than one week for vacation. He wined and dined me. We spent lazy days in bed relaxing and eating yummy cheese and fruit and toast with peanut butter. We walked along the beach and sat among the sand dunes, looking out over the ocean. It was just what I needed after the new direction my life was taking. He took me to the Hunter Valley Vineyards, and we stayed at a beautiful resort with a huge bathtub that had a TV. We had beautiful dinners and endless conversations. He was so patient with me as we drove along the countryside listening to music and stopping along the way so I could play tourist and take pictures of the beautiful scenery.

We only caught up with our mutual work friends for dinner one night. The rest of the time, we just enjoyed each other's company, so effortless and comforting. It was like I had met my long-lost best friend and soulmate. He is such a great listener, and we could easily sit in comfortable silence. One day we were hanging out, and he said "Remember how you mentioned you wanted to get married on the 28th of May originally, but then you had to choose June 4th?" I smiled and replied, "Yes," wondering where this was headed. He said, "Well, I didn't want to say anything at the time, but June 4 is the day that I married the boy's mum." Shockingly, we both started laughing at this crazy coincidence. Now, every June 4, we celebrate our non-wedding anniversary.

Our final nights were in Melbourne, the European city of Australia—alleyways full of graffiti art and coffee shops, retail stores, and high-end restaurants. We stayed at the Lindrum Hotel, room 306, and I still remember sipping champagne cocktails next to the fire in the bar area. It was all so fancy for this border town girl from Laredo, Texas. He had literally transported me to a whole other world. I'll never forget the day I jumped in the taxi to the airport to catch my flight home, crying as I rode away from him. I knew at that moment that he was my person. Luckily, he felt the same way. We figured out one of us had to move, and since he had the boys and there wasn't really anything keeping me in Texas, I decided to take the plunge. I'd taken a trip on a honeymoon credit from the wedding I never had, only to find the person I wanted to spend my life with.

We were so lucky that we both had jobs that afforded us the luxury of him making a few more trips to Austin. By November, he was meeting my parents and my huge family in Laredo. Thanksgiving lunch at my Nana's house was a big deal—there were usually about twenty-five family members attending. For a moment, I was worried when my cousins invited

Simon to the backyard to do tequila shots, but then I remembered Simon lived in Australia, and I knew he could handle his liquor—phew! And he did—he fit right in. So much so that my amazing Uncle Homer patted him on the stomach and said, "Ayyyy Samson, I like you, man." After that, he always called him Samson; it was their own little thing.

Before making the big move, I got approval from my company to spend a month in the Sydney office so I could live with Simon and just make sure I felt as good about this move as possible. Since there wasn't a role for me in the Sydney office, I had to find another job that would sponsor me. In February, I landed in Sydney with enough gear for a month, and we did a trial run. This time, I met his friends, his family, and his gorgeous boys, Liam and Oscar. The reality set in as I realized I was about to become a stepmother. This was new territory for all of us.

During that month, I found a great job with a company that sponsored my work visa. The universe was conspiring for us to be together, and everything was falling into place. I returned to Austin in March, packed up my belongings, and was back in Sydney by April for what turned out to be six and a half amazing years. I'll never forget the moment when my dad turned to me and said, "Ay mi hija, you're going international." We still laugh about that to this day. I was in my late twenties and packed all my belongings, shipping twenty-five boxes of 'stuff' through the post office. I don't know what I was thinking! I rocked up with about four or five suitcases, and Simon wondered where on earth we were going to fit everything. I had so many clothes and shoes and girly stuff. When he first leased his apartment, it wasn't intended for a girl with all this baggage. Ha! By the way, those boxes never arrived in Australia. They got held up in immigration and then shipped back to my parents' house. They didn't all arrive in Laredo either. And the boxes that did arrive were mixed up with other items that did not belong to me. Initially, I was devastated, but then I realized it wasn't a great idea to ship all my college books to Australia. Looking back, I really should have just put them in storage or let them go. I didn't know how to do that back then. Everything I owned was precious to me, even if they were material items. Up to that point, I had worked hard to accumulate my own furniture and belongings. Coming from a big family, once you learn what it's like to have your own things, you hold them dear.

Moving across the globe was a big transition. Let's just say we laid it all out on the table and discovered we had what I love to refer to as all of our sexually transmitted debt. He had been divorced for a few years and had basically started over. I had college debt and bills from being in my twenties and not being very smart with my money, purchasing all those belongings that I held so dear. Ha!

We had to learn to co-parent when we had the boys. We had them every other week and Thursday nights. We had to figure out the division of chores, cooking, and bills, and what our new life would be like together. Becoming a stepmom was exciting and scary; I always wanted to make sure to do the right thing, even though I wasn't always sure what that was! I was very self-conscious and really hoped the boys would like me and feel comfortable with me being around them. Being the oldest of seven came in handy, though, I had a very natural maternal instinct but no desire to compete or replace their mum. We decided Simon would be the disciplinarian, and I would just make sure they were safe and look out for their well-being with cuddles along the way as they got used to having me around. Being woken up by two kiddos asking to watch cartoons on Saturday mornings was new for me but easy to get used to. One of the main reasons I fell in love with Simon was because he was such a good Dad.

Of course, the boys would have normal sibling quarrels, and there were tears naturally, but for the most part, they got along really well. I grew as a person, having to not only be considerate of my partner but also of my stepsons. It had been a while since I had to consider others in the decisions and choices I was making in my life. Being used to being on my own, I had to learn to share again.

While Simon's companionship was wonderful, I had left my friends and my huge, amazing, adoring, loving, supportive family. We did not have WhatsApp or free WiFi calls. It was expensive to make overseas phone calls. We weren't as experienced using Skype, and there was no FaceTime. It was hard, and I missed my people. For extra support, I decided to continue my therapeutic journey. I didn't want to lean on Simon so much since I was new to the city and had to make new friends.

It was really important for me that we create new traditions as a family. Our first Christmas together, we went on a search for a Christmas tree and decorated it with the boys. We baked sugar cookies and exchanged gifts on Christmas morning, followed by a picnic at the beach. Christmas in the summertime was so trippy! I was used to bundling up in warm sweaters and jackets during the holiday season, not throwing on a bathing suit to have a barbeque on the beach. It really blew my mind. To this day, I still can't decide what I prefer more. We also made it a point to take the train to the city center at Martin Place every year to take pictures at the big Christmas tree, followed by gorging ourselves with chocolate at the Lindt restaurant.

We were an active little family on the weekends, sometimes going for hikes in the Royal National Park along the coastline. These are some of my favorite memories. I loved getting out into nature, spotting lizards and big bull ants, taking photos of flowers I'd never seen before and beautiful landscapes. One of our favorite spots was Little Molli Beach. It was about an hour's walk along the coastline, but once we arrived there, we'd unpack our backpacks and have a picnic with sandwiches, fruit, rice crackers, nuts, and chocolates. We'd dip our feet in the water and take a rest so we could make the journey back to the car. There was always a magpie waiting to scoop up any leftovers. Other weekends, we would take the train to the Botanical Gardens or walk around Sydney Harbour and grab a bite to eat. As the boys got older, we cheered them on at their morning soccer games before dropping them off to hang out with their friends. They grew up so fast.

Acclimatizing to living in a new country was a challenge, especially when it came to driving. It was rare to use the car because we traveled to work by train, but sometimes it was necessary for grocery shopping and other errands. Oh boy. Not only did I have to learn how to drive on the other side of the road, but I also had to learn how to navigate being on the other side of the car. I didn't even have to take a driver's test. If you have a driver's license from the US, you can get a driver's license in Australia. The roads are not as big as they are in Texas, and there are a lot of roundabouts. I started by taking a very short route to the nearest mall and practiced for a good month before slowly venturing out a little further each time. There was one time that my brother Kevin was visiting, and we were going to the North Shore, meaning I had to cross the Harbor Bridge. I was so nervous I ended up in the bus lane and didn't stop to pay the toll. Once I got home, I sheepishly walked in to announce to Simon that I'd be receiving a fine in the mail. Two hundred and fifty dollars later (yikes!!), let's just say I didn't do that again.

Being a professional in a big city requires time structure and routine. I was fairly disciplined in Austin, too, but it was different having to revolve my life around train timetables and connections. I am definitely not a morning person, so waking up early to catch a train was a big change for me.

Simon still laughs about the day that I said, "Wow, I'm really getting a lot of exercise." He was like, "What do you mean?" and I said, "Well, I have to walk to the train station (a few blocks from our apartment), then catch the train, then walk to the next train, then arrive at my destination and then walk to the office." For him, living in the city for fifteen years wasn't considered exercise, and he always laughed about this exchange. For me, coming from a place where everyone drives everywhere, that was a big deal. Let's just say I can be very lazy, so this new routine definitely took some getting used to.

One of my favorite parts of this new way of living was walking through the train stations full of shops and restaurants. Greenwood station in North Sydney was one of my favorites. At one point, Simon and I were both working in North Sydney, so we'd get there early and stop in at this adorable Italian coffee shop and order coffee and panettone. Other colleagues would squeeze in and join us to have a little visit before starting our work day. Sometimes, I'd grab a fresh cup of yogurt with figs or Turkish toast with peanut butter for breakfast. On our way home, we'd stop at what became our favorite little Italian restaurant called Capitano's and grab a Caprioska pizza and a glass of house red wine. There were butchers and fishmongers, everything was fresh, and we could just pick up groceries on our way home to make dinner. I really grew to love the train rides to and from work. On the way in, I would read, listen to music, or fall asleep on Simon's shoulder, grabbing an extra twenty or thirty minutes of sleep. It took an hour door to door. On our way home, we'd decompress from the day, sharing the highlights and lowlights; by the time we walked in the front door, we'd leave any work stresses behind to enjoy our evening.

One thing I loved about working for Australian companies was the culture. They played hard and worked hard. There was a no-nonsense approach and attitude to working. I was in my early thirties, still learning to let loose and have fun. I freaked out when my boss took me to the pub to have our 1:1s initially. Then, I quickly realized that we actually got a lot done playing pool and grabbing a pint. Employers respected the work/life balance boundaries. If you left at five o'clock to get to the gym and hop on the train to get home, they were totally cool and supportive. We had Friday happy hours in the office around three in the afternoon while reviewing the weekly sales wins, celebrating, and getting everyone amped up for the weeks ahead. This is where I first had the opportunity to build my own team. I had started off as a Salesforce administrator, and before I knew it, I had a team of five people running business systems for the sales team. Again, hats off to the mentorship and leadership I received along the way.

I never felt ambiguity in my role or my goals, and I quickly adapted to this style of doing business. I realized that this is how I like to work and operate as a human being. A no-bullshit approach where everyone is working towards a common goal to get things done. And if I made a mistake or broke something, I was supported by my leaders and colleagues. Take note that I say 'leaders' because they were not managers. They were leading by providing support, breaking down barriers, being decisive, and empowering me to get the job done. This was so refreshing coming from an American style of work culture, where I always felt everyone was competing and paranoid about losing their job or maintaining ownership of their responsibilities. I learned to work with a mentality of abundance, realizing there was always plenty of work to go around.

Most importantly, I developed friendships that would last a lifetime. There are still people we make the effort to visit with as often as possible. And if years pass between in-person visits, it doesn't matter; we pick up right where we left off. It wasn't easy at first; I had to gain people's trust and prove myself to become part of the gang. I think some people were dubious that I wouldn't last and end up going back to the States. But once they realized I was in it for the long haul, it was so much fun. To this day, I still remember my colleagues nicknaming me 'Don't mess with Texas' and 'burger' because of the way I pronounced the 'r' instead of burg-ah, which is how they all pronounced it.

As the years went by and the boys got older, we moved into bigger and bigger apartments. Our last one even had air conditioning. We started to talk about moving to Melbourne countryside, where we could afford a mortgage. Or we could move back to Texas, where the cost of living would be a 40% decrease. Of course, the decision was not easy. The boys had entered a new phase of their life, and by nature, this changed how much time we spent together. We were financially limited and felt like moving back to the US was a solid long-term plan for us. We headed back to Texas because that is where my family was, and we both loved Austin. Simon was embarking on changing careers, and we agreed that he would get his master's degree once we got settled.

Fortunately, we visited with the boys at least once or sometimes twice a year, either having them come stay with us or Simon or both of us going to Australia. Thank goodness, technology evolved just as quickly as the boys grew up. Keeping in touch with them was much easier by that time. We are all still very close as a family, and I think now even more so as they've gotten older, now in their twenties. We now meet them in London and New Zealand for the holidays. Plus, they love traveling too. Oscar is getting ready to go to Tokyo for the third time, and Liam is planning a trip to Hong Kong. They are successful, handsome young men, and I still get to cuddle with them when we visit. I hope that lasts forever!

This chapter in my life fundamentally changed me as a person. I no longer view the world through the eyes of a small-town twenty-something gal. I immersed myself in a big city, discovering diverse cultures, cuisines, nature, and exposure to an altogether different way of living. There were a few friends and family members who thought I was crazy for moving to a different country for love, for a boy nonetheless. But if I hadn't taken the leap and followed my heart, I wouldn't be the person I am today. As I've gotten older, I try to live a low-risk, no-drama life, but boy, am I glad that is not who I was in my mid-twenties. I was fearless and jumped on a plane to live in another country. As an extra perk, it's made me a really great traveler. Gone are the days of lugging around four or five pieces of luggage for an eight-day trip. I can get everything I need in one carry-on suitcase and my backpack, including three pairs of shoes.

JANENE NIBLOCK

J anene is a best-selling author and founder and chief SFDC Xpert of a woman-owned Salesforce consulting company, SFDC Xperts. With over eighteen years of operational business experience and superior knowledge of enterprise business systems, she leads a team of Salesforce experts and partners with organizations that require process automation and efficiency to accelerate growth and productivity within their workforce.

Janene lives in Austin, Texas, with my husband Simon and fur-baby Fluffy—a four-pound Chorkie and the love of her life (after her hubby, of course!). During her self-care time, she loves spending time with her hubby, sitting on the couch watching rom-coms, working on household projects, gardening, or baking sourdough bread. She also enjoys barre3, reading, listening to music, and birdwatching. Being the oldest of seven in a Hispanic family, she enjoys getting the family together for gatherings!

LinkedIn: https://www.linkedin.com/in/janeneniblock/

9

The Origins of A Solo Traveler

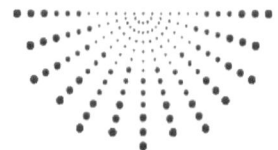

OSWALD PEREZ

T he road to being a solo traveler began with being told "no." In early 2015, my twin sister brought up that she was planning a trip to Hawaii for our thirtieth birthday in December 2015. Hawaii has long been on my bucket list for travel destinations. With visions of seeing the sunset over Waikiki Beach in Honolulu and making a visit to the volcano Mauna Loa, I couldn't ask to join the trip fast enough. But my hopes were dashed as she mentioned the words, "Girls only!"

During that same conversation, I felt a moment of bravery coming on, and I'm usually the quiet and reserved type.

I wanted to travel for my thirtieth birthday and asked my sister how I could do so on my own. She brought up the idea of "escorted travel." Previously, I'd thought that escorted tours would be for an older population, not so much for the younger generation. But we both agreed that traveling in a group would be a much safer option for me, and going on a guided tour took out all the logistics of planning the trip.

I didn't say it then, but the signs were pointing towards Spain as the destination. Why Spain? After visiting France previously, Spain was the next destination as I wanted to continue exploring the Iberian peninsula.

Then came the doubts; the first was the language barrier.

One would think that being born to a Cuban father and an Ecuadorian mother would make understanding Spanish easy, right? Not so much for me, having to use both English and Spanish, in the same home. Bits and pieces would stick. But I was worried that, being in Spain, my level of Spanish wouldn't be high enough to be in a foreign country alone.

After visiting Paris and London three years earlier, I wanted to return to Europe. Crossing the Atlantic Ocean left me enchanted, and so did the sense of being free from everything and everyone else.

In the midst of my research for the trip, I had "Don Quixote" by Miguel de Cervantes on my mind. I had borrowed a copy of the novel four years earlier from the local branch of the Queens Library. The adventures of Don Quixote and Sancho Panza amidst the scenery of windmills in Castilla de la Mancha captivated me, even if I barely finished reading the book before the library's three-week borrowing limit was done. The signs of the universe were beginning to point me in the direction of where I should be going.

On January 30, 2015, I booked a trip to Spain.

Eight days from Madrid to Seville and back. Initially, the trip was slated from November 29 to December 6, but I moved up the trip two weeks in order to avoid both of us not being home on our birthday, the first day of December.

As the winter turned to spring, I paid the trip off in full. I had not done something like this before. However, with the option to pay in installments, I could gauge the amount needed to be paid each month in order to reach the final balance. A far cry from three years earlier, as the round-trip ticket to Paris was won in a contest, and I was unemployed at the time. I paid for this trip entirely out of my own pocket, which made me feel independent and accomplished.

My second, and substantially, larger doubt was if I would be able to handle the trip.

I have cerebral palsy, and it affects my legs more than any part of my body. Would I be able to handle the hours of walking around cities, both with our guides and by myself? Would I be able to socialize with a group of people that I've never met before? Up to this point, I've traveled only with family or with friends of my sister. This situation of traveling with a group of strangers would be something that I've never experienced before. The idea of having to socialize with people terrified me due to being a quiet and reserved person. And how would I handle traveling the entire trip on my own?

As the weekend of the trip's departure arrived, there was one more wrinkle. On the night of November 13, 2015, the news showed tragic scenes from the hostage situation at the rock club Le Bataclan in Paris. That created a scenario that went through my mind of something happening to me while traveling abroad. And to a lesser extent, I wondered if the trip was going to be canceled. Thankfully, that didn't come to pass.

Sunday the 15th...departure day at last!

In the passenger seat of my dad's car, the outer edges of Queens passed by. Citi Field, the National Tennis Center, and the Queens Museum lead to one long stretch of track, the Airtrain. And then the magic words, "Welcome to John F. Kennedy International Airport," came into view. The realization that this trip was actually happening didn't hit me until I felt the plane take off and the skyline of NYC appeared in the evening's light.

At six o'clock in the morning, the morning of November 16, the trip still didn't feel real to me.

There, in the darkened light of Terminal 4S of Barajas Airport in Madrid, was a window. The white, yellow, and red stripes of the Iberia Airlines flight on one side, a reflection on the other. A long night's journey into the day was completed as I crossed the Atlantic Ocean.

The rest of the day felt like one giant blur.

From the suburbs of the airport, the transfer arrived in the city proper. I was the first person in our group to arrive at the Agumar Hotel. As I sat in the hotel lobby, a gray-haired woman with glasses came up to me and introduced herself, Judith. I didn't know that I was speaking in Spanish to our tour guide, and she understood the words that I spoke as we alternated back and forth between English. With a map of Madrid, her phone number, and the instructions to be back at six o'clock that night for the orientation, I had the rest of the day to myself. I took a quick moment to settle in my room and contact my family to let them know I had arrived safely. All of the room was mine, and the peace of mind, knowing that I had total control of the itinerary that wasn't already scheduled, more than justified paying the single supplement.

After orienting myself with the neighborhood, I found the Estacion de Atocha, where I needed to pick up my metro pass. The crystal cylinder shining in the sky stood as a memorial to the victims of the terrorist attacks on March 11, 2004. I couldn't help but wonder where else in Spain I could go with all the rolling suitcases in my sights, though my suitcase was back in the hotel room. But for now, there was plenty of Madrid to explore.

The first stop was the Museo Reina Sofia. All the walking around the art museum finally led to Room 206. And there it was, Picasso's painting "Guernica" with not another soul around. The masterwork was created in response to the Basque town of Guernika being bombed in the Spanish Civil War. Without saying a word, the sorrow could be felt. As morning turned to afternoon, it was time to get to my next stop.

For those who don't know, I'm a huge soccer fan. Watching matches on TV, playing video games, and curating a collection of soccer balls were a major part of life. And being in Madrid, there was no way that I couldn't stop at el Estadio Santiago Bernabéu, home of the fútbol club, Real Madrid. The tour began at the top of the stadium and worked its way down to the field. From sitting in the press area to the vast collection of trophies to the locker room and the field itself, I couldn't believe that I was here, even if I was standing in an empty stadium. REAL MADRID emblazoned on the seats at each end of the field, the grass, scoreboards, and the lights. This was not television or a video game; I was inside the actual stadium.

After lunch, I had time for one more destination as time and jet lag were catching up to me. I wanted to be in the center of the city. And I stepped off the metro at the station marked "Sol." As in, the Puerta Del Sol, the geographic center of Madrid and of Spain itself.

With one last stop to make, Kilometer Zero. The marker lies in front of the regional parliament headquarters. As I looked around, the picture of the Puerta on New Year's Eve being filled with people popped into my mind. I had to wait a bit for the tourists to clear up, but I had my chance. Putting both feet on the marker was a sign of good luck, and I locked it in for the trip.

That night was the orientation, a time to meet the other travelers in my group. As I had spent the day on my own, being the first person to arrive in Madrid, I was excited to see who else would be part of our group.

Introducing ourselves, it dawned on me I was the only solo traveler in our group of forty people. But everyone was so friendly, and I promptly forgot that fact. The truth remained: I was on this amazing trip that seemed like an impossibility when 2015 began, and I had such an eventful day exploring Madrid ahead.

The trip had only just begun.

The next morning at six o'clock, the phone rang—a wake-up from the front desk ushering in the first day proper. I got dressed and headed downstairs to breakfast an hour later. The buffet was a sight to behold: croissants, eggs, pancakes, yogurt, and fruit for starters. And Jamon Iberico, piles of it cut thinly sliced. As I waited in line, the red lanyards and badges with our names on them filed into the room. I said hello to as many of our group as I could and moved about the room, picking up conversations along the way. I kept looking at my watch as we had to meet Judith in the foyer by eight to begin the day of sightseeing.

Madrid awaited us as we toured the city by bus. rolling down the streets until we reached our first stop, the Plaza de España. And bringing my decision to go and visit Spain full circle was the Cervantes monument, Don Quixote riding in front and Sancho Panza behind him. In the sunny November sun, blue skies and autumn leaves circled the plaza. Another photo stop at the Palacio Real before the last leg of our tour was El Museo del Prado. Our guide, Amor, walked us through the museum, and the paintings on the walls came alive. She explained who everyone in Diego Velazquez's "Las Meninas" was, as the painting depicted King Philip the Fourth and his family. If you look closely at the painting, you can even see the artist painted himself into the artwork.

After the museum, I didn't have anything else planned for the rest of the day, so I took my own bus tour of Madrid and ended up at the last leg of the art triangle, the Thyssen Museum. The portraits of Baron Thyssen and his wife stood majestically on the second level alongside the portraits of Edvard Munch that weren't "The Scream." As I walked back to the Sol metro station, I took another moment to put both feet on Kilometer Zero to cap off the first leg of the trip.

Although we would see Madrid again before the eight-day trip ended, our next stop would take us into the southern Spanish city of Granada. But that morning, the weather gods weren't so merciful, as a deep fog rolled in on our way out of Madrid. I give our driver plenty of credit for navigating the roads when one couldn't see very far in either direction. Thankfully, we made it to our first stop of the day, Toledo, in one piece.

The fog of the morning slowly cleared out as we began our walking tour of Toledo. I felt immersed in the medieval heritage, from the city walls that surrounded me to the shops selling all kinds of medieval weapons.

A pair from Baltimore, Pat and Mike, asked me to join them for lunch. I was the only one who spoke Spanish among the three of us, so I helped them order from the menu. With glasses of house wine at the table, we began a conversation. I found out that she was a retired nurse, which made me realize why she'd been so adept at helping me over the cobbles. She checked in with me to see if I was okay, and I told her that I have difficulties staying balanced when walking on uneven terrain. Once the walking tour was over, they had asked me if I wanted to join them for lunch, and I had happily accepted the offer. While we waited for the first course to arrive, I made an effort to get to know them better. They had a pair of adult children that didn't come with them on the trip as they were traveling, and they asked me why I was on this trip by myself,and I told them that this trip was a thirtieth birthday gift. They reacted positively, saying that I was brave to travel to another country on my own.

Before we arrived in Granada, we had one more stop for this day—the town of Castilla de la Mancha. A place that reminded me of Don Quixote, as the town was patterned after the towns that Cervantes wrote about in the novel. From the windmills to the statues of Don Quixote. The late afternoon sun shone over the horizon as our brief stop led to the last stretch of road before we arrived at our destination.

As night fell, we arrived in Granada. Our guide announced a special event taking place later that night. With our tickets to the Alhambra set for the next afternoon, the opportunity arose for us to see a flamenco show in the caves outside the city. I was enthused by that prospect, even if it wouldn't happen until eleven thirty at night.

I looked out the window that night to the green and white El Corte Inglés sign lit up. I wondered in my mind how the rest of the night would've gone had I gone to the flamenco show in the Sacramonte instead of heading to bed. It was a long day on the road from Madrid to Granada, and with the stops in Toledo and Castilla de la Mancha, and the long spells on the bus, my feet were left aching. Maybe it was for the best that I went to bed, as when the morning dawned, we would be on our way to the next stop in Seville.

We had a bit of time to explore Granada before our ticketed time at the Alhambra later that morning. In the midst of the blue skies sat a sea of white-painted houses. This is the old town of Granada, the albaicin. The town is an extension of the Alhambra, the seat of the Moorish kingdom until the Spanish Reconquista of 1492. The streets were empty in the early morning hours, except for the bustling cafe that we stopped in before heading to the Alhambra.

With the help of a local guide, we explored the gardens and palaces that made up the Alhambra. I snapped photos of everything in sight. The complex was built in 1238 on the outskirts of the Sierra Nevada and was left in ruin until the early seventeenth century. Amongst the people that rediscovered the grounds, Washington Irving wrote about his experiences staying on-site for his book, "Tales of The Alhambra." In walking the three miles of the complex, it felt like I was having my own adventure in marveling at the Moorish architecture and the flora. I was left awestruck at everything that I had just seen, forgetting the fact that there was still a long afternoon's travel ahead and hours of looking at the endless meseta, the plains of Spain without the rain.

That evening, our bus delivered us to Seville under a setting sun.

Our next group dinner was around the corner from the hotel, where copious amounts of wine were served, and the conversations flowed freely, too. I found out that a post-dinner bar crawl was being planned and politely asked if I could join in. After dinner, a small group of us piled into two taxis and began the bar crawl.

If you had told me when this trip began that I would be joining in on a bar crawl, I wouldn't have believed it. Yet there we were at Bar Alfama. I also couldn't believe that I had an Estrella Galicia beer for a Euro and found my second wind just in time for the only group photo taken on the trip outside the bar. Our next stop was an interesting bar, Ruko N' Roll, which was strangely empty. Or maybe it wasn't since it was still before midnight. The bartenders served up a cocktail for all of us, but to this day, I don't know what was actually in it. All I remember was they had to use a blowtorch at the end of its creation. We arrived back at the hotel for one last stop at the hotel's bar. With a gin and tonic in hand, the clock struck midnight. I was ready to call it a night. We were exploring the rest of Seville in the morning, and I needed to rest up. As I went to bed that night, I thought to myself, this is what it feels like to be in good company. I could get used to more moments like this evening.

Friday, the 20th of November.

We began our day exploring the Andalusian capital city of Seville. And our first stop was the Plaza de Espana. The plaza is just one part of the Parque de Maria Luisa, and it was built for the Ibero-American Exposition of 1929.

Tiled benches representing every part of Spain are everywhere. When I sat down at the Catalunya bench with Barcelona written on top of it, I began to feel a tinge of regret. In two days' time, I would be flying back to New York City while some of the group would continue on to Barcelona for two more days. I would've wished for another week's stay in Spain if I could. I fell head over heels in love with everything that had already been seen so far. I wanted to see so much more of the country than we had time for in eight days. By navigating through the Jewish Quarter, we ended up at the Seville Cathedral.

It was eighty degrees in Seville in late November, which seemed crazy to think about, considering it was already autumn in New York. It made sense to have lunch outside, and as I sat at the table, the Giralda tower loomed in the distance. With my food and a glass of Mahou beer in hand, I was in a perfect frame of mind and was ready to enjoy the optional tour to come that night, a flamenco show.

At twilight, the city sparkled, leading us to the tablao, El Patio Sevillano. I had never seen a flamenco performance before. From the strums of the guitar, clapping hands, and the soulful Canto Jondo, the show made for an enlightening evening. Flamenco is a generational affair. The older women shared the stage with the young children dancing, and all of us fed off of their energy. After the show ended, I joined a small group for dinner.

Walking the streets of Seville on a warm night, the lights shined so bright. We arrived at the restaurant, San Marco, and had the back table to ourselves. As we were ordering, a miscommunication happened. I asked the waiter for a mini bottle of Codorniu cava, and he thought that I wanted the full-size bottle. Considering how kind everyone was to me over the course of the entire trip, I should've splurged and bought the table the entire bottle. I was too busy enjoying the present moment.

For the first time during our trip, the skies were cloudy and gray. But on that day, all of us had one question on our minds. Would we make it back to Madrid in time for the night's El Clasico rivalry game between Real Madrid and FC Barcelona? Two of our crew had tickets to the match that evening and had already taken the train from Seville to Madrid.

Before we made it back to the starting point of Madrid, we had one final destination to explore—Cordoba. I wasn't thinking about flying back to New York the next day, but when our guide began passing out envelopes with information for the flight home, I came back down to earth. With sadness, I realized that after all the waiting and planning, the trip was about to reach its conclusion.

Amid the palm trees burst the red and white swirls of la Mezquita de Córdoba. The site was a mosque before it became a cathedral. The arches towered over our heads as we walked through, and the light shone down on us. We had a bit of free time as we roamed, and there was a chill in the air after all the sunshine and warmth. I had one last lunch with Pat and Mike, the couple from Baltimore. Over bottles of Alhambra beer, plates of salmorejo, and white asparagus with dipping sauce, I had the chance to thank them both for their company during the trip.

The day turned to night as we arrived back in Madrid, and I couldn't run up to my room fast enough to drop my bag. El Clasico was already in progress. The rivalry between the two biggest soccer clubs in Spain also captures the attention of the world as both teams' fan bases are spread out across multiple countries. It turned out that the game was already over by the time we arrived, and Barcelona was up 4-0. But we still had time before dinner, so I sat down to watch the second half of the game live on the television screen in the hotel bar as the first half of the game had occurred during the drive from Cordoba to Madrid.

As a running joke, our guide said that she was a singer when she wasn't leading tours across Spain. Try as we did, we couldn't get her to prove that she could sing. That was until we passed by the Puerta del Sol one last time. She sang a Sephardic song, and her voice lingered in the air even if we didn't know the words to what she was singing. She wasn't kidding after all.

Together, we enjoyed one last meal at the former residence of the Duchess of Alba, which had been turned into a restaurant. I asked the two brothers who went from Seville to Madrid how their experience at the game was, and it was clear the Barcelona fan was in a happier mood than the Real Madrid one. I couldn't find them at the back table fast enough to ask how their experience was. A sold-out sea of eighty-three thousand people in the stands, tickets were going for five hundred euros each. When our bus arrived back at the hotel, the procession of goodbyes began.

Before leaving, I caught up with our guide one last time at the breakfast buffet and thanked her for all that she had done to make the trip an enjoyable experience, and we snapped one last photo.

I began the trip home the same way I arrived, on my own. Barajas is a bit quieter in the morning hours, but the parade of suitcases was numerous. I made a big mistake in packing my suitcases, as I forgot to put the large bottle of olive oil back in my checked luggage. Fortunately, I had enough time for one last duty-free stop before reaching the gate. In the shop, the Espana scarf caught my eye. It made the perfect souvenir for this trip, in addition to the bottles of red wine and sparkling wine.

I arrived at the gate and made the walk down the aisle. Sitting in my seat, and with all the demonstrations done, the wheels pulled up, and the flight back to NYC took off. I didn't want to go home, as all I could think of during the flight was why I didn't book the Barcelona extension, alternating with tears at the idea of having to return home and then go back to work. The eight days in Spain were a dream that I didn't want to wake up from.

My first solo trip had concluded. As I sat through the nine-and-a-half-hour flight home, I knew that it was not going to be the last one. Three months later, I booked the return visit to Spain for October 2016.

Traveling alone also had its challenges. I kept trying to find places to lean on or sit everywhere as I couldn't stand up for long periods of time without my feet hurting. I crashed in bed at the end of each day. Every step I took was one with caution as I could easily trip over myself if the terrain wasn't even. And for the fact that I enjoyed traveling on my own, I began to miss my family, though I emailed home at every stop. It was a grind, as we moved from city to city. All I wanted to do was stay at each destination.

Traveling alone proved that I could handle being out in the world. From navigating airports to taking the metro in Madrid and walking the streets, I did it without incident. Traveling also opened my eyes to see that I can break free from my shell and interact with the world at large, being myself without fear.

Being a solo traveler was my first step to becoming a storyteller.

OSWALD PEREZ

Oswald Perez is a writer and poet with cerebral palsy from New York City. His poems have appeared in the 2020 and 2021 editions of the literary anthology *Groundwaters*. He wrote a chapter in the best-selling multi-author book, *Authentic: Courageous Humans Who Changed Their Lives By Rewriting Their Stories*. He wrote and published a book of poems in 2020, *A Poetic Journey, Staying At Home*. He's a survivor, a late bloomer, a storyteller, a global traveler, a poet, and a writer.

Website: www.oswaldperez.com

Instagram: www.instagram.com/oswaldperez85

Substack: www.oswald.substack.com

Swell: www.swellcast.com/opwriter

TikTok: https://www.tiktok.com/@opwriter85

10

The Rising Son

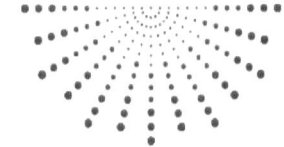

DIANA MALDONADO

Waking up from a nap on a family road trip from Texas to California, I was furious to discover that my younger brother had eaten the deliciously perfect plum I had gently placed on the dashboard, expecting to eat it later. Earlier, we had stopped at a roadside farmer's market, and looking across the bundles of fruit baskets on the tables, I carefully picked out this piece of fruit; it looked just the right size and juicy, and I imagined the joy and anticipation of savoring my plum at the right moment. Even though my father had warned my brother to eat my plum at his own peril, he did it anyway. Needless to say, my father stopped at another farmer's market to correct the sibling situation. It must have left such an impression on him since he loved retelling the story many years later with nostalgic laughter. He knew how much I wanted that plum because he recalls how meticulous I was looking through the bushels of fruit on the expansive tables.

Many years later, and under unfortunate circumstances, I found myself on the same road to California—this time, at twenty years old and with my two-year-old son, Alex. I married young, separated after two years and when it was time for a fresh start, my father came to pick us up. Excited to have us live with him, my father gleamed and opted to drive Alex and me through the Pacific Coast Highway (Highway One)—and what a ride it was! The spectacular views of the ocean, cliffs, and greenery were a stark contrast to the arid brown southwestern landscape I grew up in. After several twists and curvy turns on the highway showcased majestic views, Alex threw up in the car. What would you expect a two-year-old to do? The excitement brought us back to the reality of the passenger in tow, and we focused on the destination. Little did I know that this journey would be his springboard to travel where we would meet up later in life.

Travel was a means to an end, as I found my own space during this period. My next travel adventure with Alex took us to Mexico, where my mom lived. After my parent's divorce, she remarried and moved to Mexico. Working through guilt, shame, and a heavy burden of stress as a young mom with a two-year-old, I realized this wasn't the life I had envisioned. How did things change so quickly? Yet, being an optimist, I still managed to find a light space to take in the new places, sights, and culture. We explored caverns, waterfalls, hot springs, weekend cabin getaways, and local vibes at the markets in the Monterrey-Saltillo area. We were exploring simultaneously, and it gave me joy to share this with Alex. Seeing him enthralled with sights and culture and flowing in the moment gave me a calm that things would be OK. Seeing his sense of curiosity and wonder gave me inspiration that travel, although far from luxurious, felt like a grounding foundation from which I could embark into the unknown, especially during times of uncertainty. Releasing all caution and doubt allowed me to experience travel differently, and perhaps one day, Alex would grow up to build his own spirit of travel.

Landing at midnight in Tokyo, after a ten-hour flight, I quickly headed to the ladies' room and discovered the cleanest, heated toilet seat! It was indeed a memorable experience! I exited customs and was greeted with Alex's smile, which glowed warmly under the evening lighting of the airport. Alex, now in his thirties, moved east to travel that part of the world and found work in Hiroshima teaching English as a second language (ESL). Prior, he did a year-long ESL teaching assignment in Durango, Mexico, at a private academy, and with the teaching experience, he set his sights across the ocean. He lived there for a couple of years and would eventually live there another year. He was a sight for sore eyes, and with tear-filled eyes, I hugged him hard and was happy to see him. We got a charter bus to the hotel to settle in for the night. Looking out the window of the bus, we saw a city alive with bright lights, and I was ready for our sequel adventure.

Exhausted at the hotel and before going to bed for the night, I checked my phone messages and had a text from my sister that it was urgent. Turns out our sister-in-law, Sally, had ended a long health battle and died when I was en route to Japan. I was conflicted because I just landed from a long flight, and more importantly, I hadn't seen Alex for a long time. I acknowledged the importance of the untimely family death. After a conversation with my sister, we agreed for me to continue to visit and enjoy my time with Alex, and she would keep me posted. (In the end, I changed my return flight to visit my brother after the funeral and spend time with him and his son.)

The next day, without much haggling about what to do, Alex and I fell into a rhythm and quickly settled into a travel plan for the entire trip. Map guide in hand and our tummies filled, we set off for our first excursion, and

I questioned how we would get around and if we needed an interpreter. He casually told me, "I got this,' and puzzled, I said, "OK." To my amazement and pride, it was a delight to see Alex speak Japanese and confidently know his way through the public transit system with a totally different language in one of the largest cities in the world. I had the best tour guide! Purposely making the trip in the spring, the cherry blossoms were everywhere, and I was fascinated by how people were intentional with this natural delight by having picnics and other activities during this short-lived time of the year. We walked by the Imperial Palace, built in the 1800s, having been destroyed during World War II and now restored. Oh how serene and immaculate it looked. We followed this with a stroll through a Japanese garden, one of many throughout the city, and took in a traditional tea ceremony performed by a tea master. A wave of decompression from the long flight the day before floated away as the tea master performed with precise actions the ritual of preparing the matcha green tea with artful grace and order. After the ceremony, we wandered through the gardens, enjoying the koi fish in the ponds, cherry blossoms, and the manicured trees.

Changing the pace, we caught the subway and made our way to the ten thousand torii gates with the traditional orange color at the Hie Shrine. It was filled with winding routes, almost like a domino effect with one torii gate next to each other; all you could see were waves of orange as you would climb the endless stairs along the routes. We came upon the shrine and other burial statutes of prominence. It was a justified excuse to stop for dessert at the end of the excursion. Other fascinating stops included seeing Tokyo's far-reaching horizon from the Tokyo Tower, the pilgrimage to the Sensoji Temple, built in 645, making it the oldest temple, and taking the time to honor the rituals with the incense and bowing to fully take in the experience. Yet another breathtaking temple was the Kinkakuji or Golden

Pavilion in Kyoto, a Zen temple in northern Kyoto whose top two floors are completely covered in gold leaf. The marvel of a temple in the middle of a pond with gold glittering against the water was a sight to see. We ventured by train an hour outside Kyoto to the countryside to Nara, where we enjoyed a host of cultural treasures and the largest temple, Todaiji Temple, which houses the largest bronze Buddha. Nara was the capital back in 710, but with the Buddist monks gaining power, the capital was moved to Nagaoka. Walking quietly among the tourists, we peered through massive proportions of the temple outlined with intricate designs and came out to the tranquil park with tame, gentle deer that are considered sacred, so they roam freely with the tourists and would eat from your hand the deer snacks for sale at the park. This was truly a zen moment!

Tokyo was buzzing with so much stimulation for the senses—from the three-story animation ads to the overwhelming lights and the Shibuya Crosswalk noted as one of the busiest crosswalks in the world. Taking in the sea of human crossing, it was all done in uniformity, from caricature wardrobe trends to a quiet place in the middle of the city, participating in a tea ceremony. Traveling with Alex was a unique and bonding experience that I cherish because although I traveled to know a different part of the world and culture, it was in this space I got to know him as an adult and friend, and it turns out we were great travel partners. He got the wanderlust travel bug, too!

Like clockwork, every morning, we would wake up at seven o'clock sharp, take a few minutes to go over the plan from the night before, get ready, and head out the door. Our collective sweet tooth was surprisingly met with French bakeries as that was the new eating trend in Tokyo. Throughout the day, Alex kept an eye out for local eateries along the way, and one of the many stops was a restaurant where sushi was placed on a rolling conveyor belt. Seeing the train of so many selections of sushi being prepared in front of you was a fun experience, and seeing Alex talk to the chef was entertaining. With our full bellies, we trekked along to the next adventure. We'd stop in for pastries between our extended walks throughout the city, going in and out of subways and walking to new destinations. Our subway and train rides took us to Kyoto, Osaka, Nara, each beautiful, with deep history and culture. I think I walked around with my mouth wide open with such amazement at the intricacy of art, food, and way of life. The conformist way of life lent a rhythm to the throngs of people everywhere. The beige, black, white wardrobe ensembles with satchels in tow on the subways and sidewalks whispered for you to flow in with the crowd. Exhausted at the end of each day, I went to sleep with a deep smile, knowing I was experiencing this moment with my son and how proud and impressed I was to see him as a translator and guide.

Gliding on the famous bullet train, the fastest train in the world, also had its light rhythm as we enjoyed our last day together. Alex had brought along his backpack and initially said he would be taking a train back to Hiroshima. But it didn't really hit me that we would go our separate ways at the end of this excursion. And then it really sunk in! He explained that he had to go back home to Hiroshima, which was around five hours from Kyoto, and it would make sense for him to go home from here, and I, in turn, would travel by myself on the bullet train back to Tokyo. Of course, I started to panic because I couldn't read the signs and made several excuses. But more importantly, I wasn't ready to let him go. I paused for a long moment and looked around the train station among the throngs of people bustling to and from their busy day. It was the loudest noise yet so quiet as I contemplated the next moment. It had been a long time since I had seen him, and who knew how long it would be when I would see him again.

Inevitably, I sighed in agreement and agreed it was the practical thing to do. Going over the directions on a note card he had prepared, he directed me with step-by-step instructions on how to get to Tokyo and back to my hotel. He said to look for the subway attendants, and they would steer me in the right direction. Filled with emotion, I tearfully said goodbye, and a thought came to me of our roles reversed. There I was, like a little girl getting ready to board the school bus, being reassured by Alex, when many times I did this for him when he was little. It's funny how travel has no boundaries or layers of order; it simply is for those who choose to flow in this path of freedom!

So, I boarded the bullet train, and true to his word and notes, I flagged down a guide to make sure I was going in the right direction, and with broken English, he confirmed the note card Alex had written for me was correct. I made it back to my hotel ready to fly out the next morning.

On my long flight home, I cried silently in my seat. I was filled with so much emotion because the trip was more than just a trip. Travel allowed me to connect with my son in a totally new and fun way and to see his beautiful and kind spirit shine again at a time earlier when it had been dimmed due to life challenges. Travel was a way for me to grow stronger and deeper with my kids because, as a young mother, I know there were many gaps, and with this new chapter of life, it is amazing how far we travel to deepen and embrace our relationships with the people most special in our lives. Alex opened that door for me to pause and slow down to the beauty and wonder through his eyes. While I thanked him, I don't think he really knows how much this centered me on how I would experience travel moving forward. I used my time on the flight to go through the collage of photos and created a slideshow of this once-in-a-lifetime experience.

A couple of years later, with Alex now living in Thailand, we ventured into the aggressive streets of Bangkok on a tuk-tuk to get to the Grand Palace, ate the best mango sticky rice from a street vendor, and yet again, he had scoped out good places to eat. The most memorable time was when we boarded a small passenger plane to the Krabi Islands and sailed along the Andaman Sea on a tour boat and came upon the most stunning scenery of cliffs jutting out from the sea. Jumping into perfect temperature-turquoise water with colorful fish floating around us felt like heaven on earth. The day ended with a feast on pristine white beaches and a bonfire to top off the evening.

After Alex finally moved back to the States, our travels have taken us hiking in Yosemite, with good restaurants along the way. Even now, as I am preparing for the Tokyo 2024 marathon, he is on board to travel with me. Another chapter awaits in the wings, and I can't wait for it!

With practice, going places and booking flights has become easier, and my world has expanded with the wonders of the globe and culture. I find myself being at peace more and more, and my work flourishes because I use my travel experience to find solutions instead of being mired in problems. Travel has become a way I choose to live intentionally, and it makes me appreciate the beauty and simplicity that daily life offers.

Thinking back on the plum episode—oftentimes as I am in transit, I reflect on that first long trip to California and how I can now fill in the blanks of the questions I asked back then. Would my travel expand, and who would I share it with? What lessons and gifts would come from the adventures in travel?

I could never have known that the answers to these questions are that one day, I would travel the world and run global marathons in Berlin, London, and Paris. I would hike in Patagonia and see the majestic condor and walk on a glacier, run in the Sahara and lunch with a nomad family, and hike through the Julian Alps in Slovenia and along the Adriatic Sea in Croatia. That summer ride in the back seat formed a foundation to see nature, people, food, and culture and embrace the diverse way humanity thrives and struggles.

As a curious young Latina with a strong spirit for adventure, I learned to use travel as a way to balance life's successes and potholes, embrace beautiful experiences, and share them with the special people in my life. I am forever grateful for Alex's spirit and curiosity and that, as my son, he helped me answer my questions. The intertwining of these always beckons for an adventure. Travel will always be that fruit I gently place on the dashboard, and I get to take a bite and savor it every time I pack my bags to my next destination—carefully chosen, greatly anticipated, and always deliciously juicy.

DIANA MALDONADO

D iana Maldonado is a best-selling author and CEO of Maldonado Strategies. As a long-time Austin political figure, she helps organizations design and implement innovative solutions to accelerate vision goals using her insight for pinpointing incongruences and listening.

As the first Latina elected to represent Williamson County in the Texas House of Representatives, Diana has a record of accomplishing the "impossible" while building lasting relationships. She is passionate about helping women run for office—and succeeding when they get there. Diana is a global marathon runner and feng shui enthusiast, and loves spending time with her three-year-old granddaughter, Camila.

Facebook: www.facebook.com/diana.maldonado.39566

LinkedIn: www.linkedin.com/in/diana-maldonado/

Website: https://www.maldonadostrategies.com/

11

Excavating the Goddess Warrior: A Journey Back to Myself

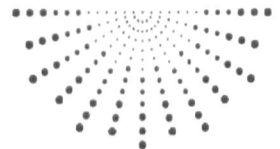

SUSIE MOCERI

My life, really, began with a plane ride across the world in January of 1980. I was two-and-a-half years old when I left the orphanage and took the fourteen-hour flight from Seoul, South Korea, to JFK Airport in New York to meet my adoptive family. I have no memory of my time in Korea and don't even have a birth certificate; my birthday is a random date assigned based upon my physical development. Only one picture exists of my time there—the one sent to prospective parents.

Occasionally, I look at that black and white photograph, into the eyes of a young girl, a girl who I view almost as a stranger, a ghost from my past. The people who cared for her, the experiences she had, even the food she ate, are as foreign to me as any other little girl who lived on the other side of the world would be. And so, my arrival to my family in the United States marks the start of my life, the initial point where my memories begin, and albums of photographs document my childhood, memories, and growth.

Adopted into a family with financial means, I was fortunate to vacation frequently as a child. Through my childhood vacations to places like Guadeloupe, the Bahamas, Spain, Mexico, Belize, Honduras, and Hawaii, the greatest lessons I learned were to admire other cultures, to appreciate the fortunate lifestyle in which I was raised, and simultaneously learn from people who led more simple lives. Growing up in Long Island and enduring the frigid, gray, and bleak winters, I always looked forward to our frequent visits to tropical locations. The exposure to those places cultivated my love for warm weather, turquoise water, a glowing sun, fresh fruits, and just-caught seafood (there is nothing quite like witnessing a local fisherman in the Bahamas produce a fresh conch and prepare a conch salad before devouring the chopped bits mixed with onions, peppers, jalapeño, cilantro, and the juices from an orange, lime, lemon—a finished dish that is briny with a hint of heat but is overall a burst of fresh flavor. I have visions of when I will return for more.).

However, underneath the façade of my upper-middle-class family with a waterfront home, luxury cars, boats, private schools, and tropical vacations, I silently guarded a terrible truth.

My father had molested me for as long as I could remember, my earliest memory occurring from when I was around five years old. Throughout my early childhood, I lived in a vague, confusing, paralyzing state of anxiety, fear, and an indescribable sense of insecurity within what superficially seemed to be a desirable, stable, even blessed life. I remained silent, too afraid to reveal what was happening to me, too frightened by the potential ramifications if I uttered the truth. As an adult, I came to realize that my silence and anxiety were likely compounded since I was adopted, which added an unconscious layer of fearing another abandonment. Furthermore, my mind rationalized that he wasn't my biological father, which somehow diminished the transgression.

For several years, my family vacationed at Club Med in Guadeloupe during the winter. Teachers provided my brother and me with a packet of work to complete during our two-week absence from school amidst all the fun activities of the children's camp, such as snorkeling, water skiing, archery, and crafts. It was here I came close to telling my mother about my abuse.

Club Med resorts boast nighttime entertainment, and the children's camp prepared various performances. During this particular trip, one skit included several of us girls, ranging in age from perhaps five to eight years old, portraying girls in a canoe with Polynesian music in the background, a hula dance of some sort. The night of the performance, I discovered backstage that my costume consisted solely of a grass skirt and lei. No top. I froze, and tears started to fall down my face as I refused to go on stage. The idea of standing half-naked publicly in front of my father was horrifying and simply not going to happen. I recall my mom being called backstage and her encouraging me to participate, emphasizing how my six-year-old body wasn't yet developed, and besides, the women in Guadeloupe went topless on the beaches.

But I continued to weep, sliding down the wall until I was huddled into a ball, folded into myself until the skit was over. Gleeful and tipsy parents cheerfully applauded their little ones' performance while I felt isolated and pained despite being on this beautiful tropical island. I remained silent, unable to share the truth, not yet possessing the strength to self-advocate, something I wouldn't develop until many years later.

"Wherever you go, there you are" is a Buddhist reflection that, in part, emphasizes the importance of mindful awareness in the present moment. But it also identifies the unavoidable truth that we always carry the entirety of our life's experiences with us. No amount of denial or running to escape a problem will negate that it happened or its impact. No amount of surface-level glitz, glamor, sparkles, or smiles will erase the unhealed wounds that exist internally. Lavish trips with luxurious accommodations in dazzling locales could not be fully appreciated until I tackled my trauma head-on through an abundance of self-work. Achieving harmony between beautiful surroundings and internal tranquility would take a number of decades.

It wasn't until about twenty-five years after that particular trip to Guadeloupe that I finally disclosed the truth to my mother. After my parents had divorced. After, I suppose, I felt a new sense of security in my own marriage (flawed, as it turns out to have been) and starting a family of my own.

I met my husband when we were both in our twenties and living in Los Angeles. We enjoyed the perfect weather of Southern California, endless days of sunshine with temperatures in the 70s and 80s. His apartment was two blocks up from the beach with sweeping views of the glistening Pacific. Those were mostly carefree years while we dated, full of parties with friends, rollerblading along The Strand, eating and drinking at all the restaurants and bars on the Hermosa Beach Pier, whipping around the hills of Palos Verdes in my convertible, top down, tunes blasting, the sun kissing my bare shoulders.

He was a corporate attorney at a large firm at the time, and in the fall of 2003, he went to their London office to work on a deal. A couple of days before Thanksgiving, he texted me: "If I get you a ticket, can you fly here tomorrow for the weekend?" Although spontaneity is not generally in my nature, this last-minute trip was a romantic gesture I couldn't ignore. He told me he would be working when I arrived, but upon checking in at The Lanesborough, a five-star hotel, our personal butler would make sure I settled into our room.

It was a whirlwind few days that included dinner at the world-famous (although now closed) Simpson's in the Strand, where the servers carved their signature prime rib tableside on the trolley. We saw *Mama Mia!* at the Prince of Wales Theatre, a fantastic and fun performance that concludes with the audience getting up and dancing, belting out the lyrics along with the actors to "Mama Mia," "Dancing Queen," and "Waterloo." Another night, as we wandered around Covent Garden, a sidewalk musician began singing "Here Comes the Sun," and my boyfriend swept me in his arms, serenading me as we swayed together under the moonlight. I had visions of the type of luxurious vacations we would have once we were married, never giving thought to what travel would look like after having our four children – let alone as the uncoupled co-parent I would eventually become.

A seasoned parent clarified for me the difference between a *trip* with young children versus a *vacation* that is truly relaxing. There is no semblance to the freedom, ease, and pace that exists when you are a solo traveler. Now that my kids are older, we no longer have to haul strollers and diaper bags, sending discreet, apologetic looks to annoyed travelers in the security lines, but traveling as a family of six (and quite often more with extended family, a nanny, or friends joining) requires an abundance of preparation, patience, and flexibility.

From the beginning of parenthood, my husband and I traveled with our children. My oldest was three months old when we flew with her from Austin, Texas, to Detroit, Michigan, for her baptism and celebration. We have since brought the children to Michigan several times to visit paternal relatives, to Laguna Beach to escape the Texas summer's oppressive heat, to Cabo for beachy vacations, to Colorado for ski lessons, to Maine for an exposure to the Atlantic and a more rustic experience, and, of course, to Disney World, to meet Mickey and the gang—deliberately choosing destinations we could reach on non-stop flights.

When my oldest reached two years old, I couldn't help but look at her in complete awe at how she was undoubtedly her own little person with a distinct personality, an affinity for order and organization, a quiet yet ever-observant gaze, and already a sweet tooth.

I was her age when I entered the orphanage in Korea. I couldn't imagine the impact it would have on my beloved child if she were placed in an institution with strange adults and children and, within months, flown to a country on the other side of the world where everyone looked different, spoke a foreign language, ate unfamiliar food, and was placed in a home with strangers as her new family. Looking at my child's innocent face and feeling her complete trust in me brought back to my mind's eye the image of the black and white photograph of me as a two-year-old in Korea: the sadness, the stoicism, the resolve that already appeared in my countenance and posture—a seed of strength perhaps already visible.

Today, I marvel at how far that little girl has traveled, both literally and figuratively.

In the summer of 2016, my daughters were two, three, and four years old when we took our first two-week trip to Laguna Beach (my son would be born the following year). With my youngest clinging to me the entire time, I returned home to Austin with an injured back that required three weeks of chiropractic treatment. She was a two-year-old beast of a girl at the time, which I truly say lovingly. Her godmother, my cousin, aptly dubbed her a "wrecking ball" when she was only one year old, for she would fling herself into you for an embrace. Trust me, it fits. At that time, she weighed more than her older sister of seventeen months, and she bruised me on an almost daily basis.

During that trip, sleep eluded me. Not only because my littlest one demanded to sleep with me but because, apparently, a year shy of forty years old, I had reached the age where I could no longer sleep on lumpy mattresses. With her sharing my bed, my husband found respite in a separate bedroom, a sleeping arrangement that was becoming increasingly common, much to my disappointment and growing concern. The house was silent with everyone asleep, but something thrummed within me in response to the crashing waves outside, and in the darkness, I typed out this poem in an iPhone note in the middle of the night:

Flung

Rolling waves are supposed to be soothing.
But these Pacific monsters are accosting.

Aggressive.
Disturbing.
Disruptive.

A maelstrom of power.
  Relentless.
Swirling currents and riptides
  pulling,
yanking,
  ripping me from the safety of the shore.
Into the pounding,
  beating,
unforgivable cycle of give and take,
  high
and
low tide.

The briefest of peace
in
the

second

or

two

before the next barrage.

Beautiful, hold-your-breath calm—
Interrupted.
By the expected,
 Inevitable,
Impending surge.

I yearn
for the gentle lapping
of the Gulf Coast,
the turquoise of the Caribbean...

The Lone Palm.

The whistling of palm fronds and
Casuarina.

Four years later, when my daughters were six, seven, and eight years old, and my son was three, the other shoe finally dropped. Until that point, our thirteen years of marriage and parenthood appeared perfect, with more than one friend telling me they were honestly—although obviously thrilled for me—a little bit jealous about my life: my healthy and thriving children and my ability to be a stay-at-home mom. My husband had bravely left his firm right after we got married and started his own company, which grew quite successful over the years, allowing us a privileged lifestyle. But in 2020, I filed for divorce. It had taken several years for me to reach the point where I gained enough strength to pull the trigger and move forward in that decision. In reality, throughout our marriage—despite a seemingly beautiful, successful, and happy family and relationship—secrets were again coursing underneath the surface. What was superficially shiny held an ugly truth below.

Over the years, tiny questions led to mounting hints, and raised eyebrows became red flags. Ultimately, undeniable evidence overcame his gaslighting and my willful denial. Laguna's disturbing, crashing waves were a harbinger for what was to come: being beaten down by an onslaught of painful information, a period of suffering I had not known prior, and my yearning for courage and peace.

I couldn't sleep.

I didn't eat.

I cried.

I wailed.

I raged.

I retreated and hibernated.

And then I wandered through days, weeks, and months, a shadow of myself, floating mindlessly through the seconds, minutes, hours of my motherly duties, all while feeling destroyed and betrayed. I was a shell, numb, hollowed out from the grief and the pain.

Years earlier, during the time my husband and I were trying to start a family and facing difficulty in doing so, he encouraged me to seek therapy to heal from the trauma of my childhood sexual abuse. Denial is a deeply rooted, self-preservation tool. Finally confronting how the years of denial and silence damaged my sense of security, and finally acknowledging I could now choose my path forward, I was able to sever all contact and communication with my father. Mind, body, spirit: harmony among the three is mysterious yet paramount. I do not think it is a coincidence that the month after I uninvited and excised my father from my life, I became pregnant after years of trying and without any fertility assistance.

Now, faced again with a pain I could not reconcile alone, I resumed therapy sessions. Those appointments were a lifeline, an hour carved out in the week when I knew I could crumble in a safe space, be heard, and receive exceptional guidance. Those meetings helped fortify me to survive the week until the next one.

Days, weeks, and months passed, yet I observed the outside world as if I were detached, buffered in my own cocoon. Everyone else appeared to move quickly throughout the day, bouncy with cheer, while I felt every movement of mine was met with resistance, and there was a barrier that muffled any sound or connection between me and anyone else.

At the recommendation of my therapist, I read Glennon Doyle's *Love Warrior*. I wept as I read her story, but by the end, I started to feel a spark of hope. During this time, a meme came across my Facebook feed that said, "Pain makes a woman a warrior." So meaningful were Doyle's book and this phrase that soon after, I headed to Gully Cat Tattoo on South First Street in Austin and tattooed the Japanese kanji for "Warrior" on the inside of my right wrist.

Several months later, I was talking to one of my closest friends of twenty-five years. She is the type of friend who not only listens—listening to hear and not to respond, being a safe receptacle for my thoughts and emotions—but she also shares insight, wisdom, and encouragement. Sara told me she loved the idea of my tattoo, but she said, "Susie, you are not just a warrior. You are a Goddess Warrior."

Oh. My. Goodness. The moment she said that phrase, the hairs on my arms and neck stood up. Those two words spoke to my core, and I knew a part of me had finally been named. While I had started to build my inner strength back up, and my tattoo was a literal branding of this side of me, the *Goddess* qualifier elevated this aspect of myself to not just an agent of strength in war but a softer vehicle of the divine—a fighter, but also a deliverer of peace.

Not only had I been talking extensively with my therapist, but I had also signed up for a Clarity writing course with parenting coach Carrie Contey, PhD, who I call my life guru. Working with both of these professionals led me to focus on listening to the internal Knowing, the source of wisdom, the quiet voice who discerns the truth. Amid swirly thoughts and feelings, when we are able to slow down and drop into our Gut, there is always the answer, even if it may be obvious or surprising, comforting or scary.

I discovered that I could identify a number of instances in my life when I had listened to that instinct, resulting in desired outcomes, or I had ignored that voice with disastrous results. That inner Knowing, for me, was The Goddess Warrior, the part of me I had squelched and silenced the majority of my life. I had not wanted to listen to her, too afraid to disrupt the status quo, too terrified to confront the unknowns in fear of causing a stir.

Months and years passed as I continued working with my therapist and journaling through multiple Clarity courses. My therapist suggested I try an alternative therapy session using a proscribed combination of psilocybin and MDMA, recommending I complete my due diligence into the Multidisciplinary Association for Psychedelics Studies (MAPS) clinical trials in using psychedelics to treat PTSD. I read many articles and watched a number of videos MAPS produced, as well as spotlight news stories on the subject, and decided to give the treatment a try.

Since I had never consumed any psychedelics before, I was nervous and unsure of what to expect. After drinking the psilocybin tea and lying on the practitioner's couch, I began to see a kaleidoscope of images on the wall. At first, it was a neon light show of mandalas and lotuses, followed by pulses of obscured faces. One female face, in particular, continuously reappeared among all the other morphing ones. Hers was also unclear, but I felt she held significance. Who was she? Was she my biological mother? I felt like she was me but also not me. She emanated strength, confidence, and beauty. Hours passed, and, eventually, only that woman's face remained.

All other images had disappeared, and her face stilled, becoming clear. A bursting awe yet sublime peace washed over me.

The face was mine.

It was The Goddess Warrior revealing herself, communicating that she would be inhabiting my body with more space. I had spent years of therapy and journaling trying to rebuild my broken spirit, heal my shattered heart, and restore my damaged confidence. While my mind had started to acknowledge the positive characteristics I possessed, deep down, I did not fully believe those things; rather, I subconsciously believed that I was unattractive, undesirable, weak, and unworthy of love.

It was an unmatched transcendent experience, this moment in which I knew I could trust in myself. Much like Dorothy at the end of *The Wizard of* Oz, I realized I had always already possessed everything I ever needed and didn't need to search for external validation or accept unhealthy love.

I had successfully excavated The Goddess Warrior, and I knew my life would be taking a different path going forward. My ex-husband might be a brilliant, successful businessman and CEO, but I, too, was a force to be reckoned with.

My conscious intention was to navigate the divorce process with as much grace and dignity as possible. We did not even tell our children about it until almost a year after I had filed because we wanted to determine which direction it would go—would we be civil with each other, or would it become the next world war?

We were in the midst of the Covid crisis, locked down at the house. However, as time wore on and restrictions were lifted, we continued to celebrate everyone's birthdays and holidays together. Trick-or-treating as a family in my in-laws' neighborhood, our dog Maximus in tow, Mother's and Father's Day, Thanksgiving, and Christmas were all celebrated with extended family. The world was experiencing a pandemic, and so we focused on keeping whatever we had the power to control as stable as possible for the children.

My ex-husband and I showed up to all the Little's special events together: First Reconciliation, First Communion, soccer games, piano recitals, basketball games, and track meets. A close mom friend of mine at the school who knew about the divorce told me other moms were whispering, confused about whether my ex and I were getting divorced or not, since we attended school events and sat together.

Throughout the year-and-a-half process for the divorce to be finalized, my goal was to keep the children's lives as undisrupted as possible. We began "nesting," with the Littles staying in the house. The ex and I acquired our own separate residences and took turns with the children on a weekly basis.

We continued to take family trips, both together and separately. He took them with the nanny to Colorado to ski, and I took them with a friend and her daughter to The Atlantis in the Bahamas for New Year's (and yes, I did get a conch salad, but not nearly enough servings!). We all revisited Disney World and Universal Studios in July 2022 with his parents, and a month later, we flew to one of our usual spots in Cabo, again with my in-laws.

When Spring Break 2023 approached, we decided to return to Cabo once again. However, his parents, our nanny, and various friends were unavailable to join us, leaving us to travel together, just the six of us. I don't remember the last time we traveled with the children without any outsiders.

The trip went smoothly; he and I were—dare I say not just civil but actually friendly—and I could tell the children appreciated the different dynamic of being with just their parents, and they saw that we could indeed continue to operate and exist as a family unit. Perhaps it was a bit confusing as they asked several times why we couldn't continue living under the same roof, my oldest daughter even offering to give up her room and share a bedroom with one of her sisters so we could each have our own rooms.

Flying back from Cabo, presumably because the trip went so well, my ex asked what I thought about possibly taking an extended trip to Europe during the summer, where we would maintain our week-on/week-off schedule. I asked him to let me consider it. Some days later, I suggested we make this trip similar to our last family trip together—that we could start with a week together, I would then take them for a week, he would take them for a week, and then we would finish the trip with a week all together again. He agreed it was a good idea, and we began planning the details.

Most people are stunned to hear we travel together post-divorce, particularly after enduring such a painful phase in the marriage. Our children are still young, and we have many more years of co-parenting ahead of us, so we had to find a way to make this work. The Goddess Warrior in me knows that bitterness and retribution serve no one in this scenario, and this truth drives how I try to interact with my ex.

And so, we experienced a five-week marathon European adventure this summer. Together, we took the children to London and Paris. From there, I took the Littles to Cannes, Barcelona, and Madrid while he spent his ten days "off" gallivanting around a variety of Italian cities. My in-laws joined the children and me in Madrid and then flew with them to meet up with their father in Rome and explore Florence.

I had planned my ten days sans children in Mykonos, Greece, inviting three of my closest friends to join me, women who are ten to fifteen years older than me but whose wisdom, strength, and kindness drew me to them so many years ago. It warmed my heart that they so quickly and easily jumped at the opportunity to meet up halfway across the world: one from Austin, the second from Florida, and the third from Puerto Rico.

My friends and I enjoyed lazy days lounging by our pool, reading, chatting, choking on giggles, and taking in the breathtaking, sweeping view of the sparkling Aegean Sea with spectacular yachts and sailboats dotting the bay under the blazing sun. We chartered a sailboat to swim at Reina and explore the ruins of Delos, rode a high-speed ferry to Paros, shopped the boutiques through the winding paths of town, and ate fresh Mediterranean cuisine at every turn.

Most importantly, we shared updates in our lives, laughed over memorable times from the past, and confided our hopes and fears—personal details of our marriages, new relationships, dreams for our children, and managing our aging parents. These three women were there for me during one of the darkest periods of my life when my marriage disintegrated, and to celebrate with them this summer as I have emerged years later stronger and wiser felt triumphant and joyful.

The Goddess Warrior apparently also possesses some sassiness. Although she is poised and articulate, she is proud to wear—after birthing and raising four babies—daring bikinis and sexy, backless dresses with plunging necklines. She demands honesty and clarity in all of her interactions. *Doing* and *spending* however I pleased post-divorce was the most liberated I have ever felt in my entire life.

I—finally—didn't have to answer to anybody but myself.

And it just tickled me, making me swell with pride and gratitude for all I had endured, survived, and conquered. How far I had come.

As a whole, the trip was a beautiful balance of family time together, my solo time with the Littles, and also a much-needed reunion—a *vacation* amidst the *trip*—with three women who fed my soul. Unlike so many of my prior travels, where I felt compelled to paint a smile on my face to match my beautiful surroundings, this time, my inner peace and joy equaled the glorious brightness of Mykonos.

I still pull out that black-and-white photo of myself in Korea from time to time. I peer into the shadows of her two-year-old eyes, an image captured forty-four years ago. And I reach out to her. The Goddess Warrior extends her arms and enfolds that child into a tender embrace.

SUSIE MOCERI

Susie Moceri discovered her passion for writing and reading at a young age and has been honing her craft ever since. With a BA in English and an M.Ed. from the University of Florida, Susie explores themes of race, identity, love, and the complexities of the human experience in her writing. After college, Susie pursued her childhood vocational dream in the class-room, guiding and inspiring eleventh and twelfth grade students, fostering critical thinking, analytical writing, and a deep appreciation for literature. When not immersed in the world of words, Susie is busy raising her four children, being active in their school community and philanthropy, and making time to play with her one-year-old Yorkie puppy.

Facebook: www.facebook.com/susie.estabrook

Instagram: www.instagram.com/estabrooksusie

12

Tiny Footprints in China

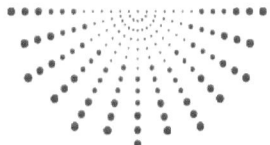

KALPASHREE GUPTA

"Wherever you go becomes a part of you somehow" – Anita
Desai

Standing at the top of the Great Wall of China in 2015 with Arnab by my side and Aryan in the baby carrier close to my chest, I felt free and in awe. My cheeks felt warm in the freezing cold, and I basked in the radiance of the sun shining above us. Our close family friends and my colleagues, Shaily and Kaushik, aka KB, Basu, had joined us on our China trip. As I stood there admiring the view, I saw them walk further ahead and climb a steep section with hundreds of stairs at the Wall. Seeing them near the top, I had an urge to join them, but my heart yearned for me to be still. I was exhilarated, yet tired, and I could feel my heart throb. I do recall walking a lot with Aryan in my baby sling, mostly ahead of everyone else, and I needed to catch my breath. My mind started projecting the previous three decades of my life like a black-and-white movie. I wasn't just standing on the Great Wall of China; I was also standing upon the shoulders of my family who'd given me both the resiliency and wanderlust that had brought me to this place.

As far as I can remember, my wanderlust began at an early age. When my brother was a toddler and I was nearly four, my parents embarked on a month-long bus trip with my dad's colleagues and their families. We covered a dozen cities across five states, starting from our home in a rural mining town (Saunda D Colliery) in Bihar (now the state of Jharkhand) in Eastern India and traveling all the way to Southern India. This was a simple trip. The bus tickets were provided for free for our family in exchange for my dad bringing business (the travelers) to the travel agent; the entire trip cost a total of 5,000 rupees for our family, which was nearly two months of my dad's salary.

I may have been too young to retain any memories of our month-long bus trip. Yet, I remember the vivid image of Vivekananda Rock in Kanyaku-mari, the southernmost tip of India. This was a monument honoring Indian philosopher, author, and monk Swami Vivekananda, who's famous for his speech introducing Hinduism in the Parliament of World's Religions in Chicago in 1893. The water gushing against the rocks and a pedestrian bridge connecting the memorial—I had never seen such an expanse of water as this one before. That body of water, the Lakshadweep Sea, borders three countries—Maldives, Sri Lanka, and India. The Arabian Sea, Bay of Bengal, and the Indian Ocean meet right there. It is also said that Vivekananda found enlightenment on one of the two rocks after meditating for three days. Gazing at the indestructible rocks in that endless sea, I wonder if travel was a way for the universe to pass down resiliency to me. The portraits of Swami Vivekananda also adorned the walls of our home, and my family greatly revered him.

My grandparents migrated from the state of West Bengal to Bihar and were the source of strength, love, learning, and spiritual connection in my life. It is remarkable how my great-grandmother, Sarojini Gupta, who didn't have any formal education, used to write poems to inspire freedom fighters in pre-independent India. She was widowed at a young age with three young children and raised them well. I feel blessed that she was alive for the first eight years of my life. I only felt pure love from her, despite the hardships she faced throughout her life.

My maternal grandmother, Panchami Roy, lost both her parents at a young age—I don't know how her dad died, but I heard that her mom died of hunger while fasting for two days in the summer months. Once, my mom found my grandma with a fever sitting by her tiny kitchen window, waiting for her extended family members to pass by in the alley so she could borrow a meager ten rupees to feed her three children. Witnessing the helplessness of her mom at a young age had a profound effect on my mom, and she grew up to become one of the most generous people I know.

My maternal grandfather was a librarian in the public library in Bhamuria, a village in West Bengal. During our annual summer trips to the village, I honed my Bengali by reading Bengali books from the village library. Education was part of our culture, and my parents and other family members worked diligently to pass on that value to me.

At sixteen, unlike most of my friends, I moved away from my family for higher education as we didn't have good colleges in my hometown. I lived in Kolkata, Delhi, and Bangalore for school and work for the next decade. Although my early education was in a Catholic school, the primary medium of instruction was always Hindi. When I moved away to Kolkata, learning to speak in English to communicate with friends in the girls' hostel where I lived was one of my most profound experiences. This is where I met my best friend, Meiyu, an incredible woman of Goan and Chinese heritage. My friends Meena and Maliha, who helped me acclimate, whether it was helping me relearn math or science in English in high school or inviting me over for a home-cooked meal in college, remain closest to my heart, and we are still connected to this day.

At the time of this China trip, Arnab and I had been married for close to nine years. He came to the US as a student right before 9/11 to attend the University of Texas at Austin. After graduation, he settled in Phoenix for his first job. I graduated from the Delhi School of Economics and was working with GE in Bangalore when we first met each other.

Although the story of our first meeting is a usual one, like most Indian couples who meet through family or matrimonials, what surprised me at the time was that "I" was going through an arranged marriage. I was very independent, but my parents refused to share my phone number with his family, and I didn't find out about that until years later. My parents called me one day and asked me to visit home during the Durga Puja holidays so we could all visit my cousin's place in Jamshedpur (a few hours' drive from where my parents lived) and so I could meet a potential suitor, an alumnus of the Indian Institutes of Technology (IITs) who was visiting his parents from the US. I was recovering from a broken heart and exhausted by yet another arranged marriage attempt. I grudgingly agreed, fully intending to say no after meeting the suitor. God must have laughed at my plans.

In our first meeting, I saw simplicity and sweetness, literally, as he walked into a room full of my relatives and handed me a pack of chocolates. Disregarding our family norms, later that night, I coached my dad to call Arnab's dad (only if my dad really wanted us married) and convey to him that "I" wanted to meet Arnab alone this time. My dad called him right away, and I laugh about that conversation to this day, remembering the hesitation on his face when he made that phone call. They agreed to a second meeting the next day. Two interactions later, I said yes to marrying Arnab, as I felt I could trust him and live with him. An added bonus: he loved cooking! Eight months later, we exchanged vows. I quit my job in Bangalore, moved to Phoenix, and embarked on a fresh chapter at Thunderbird School of Global Management to study business.

Resigning from my job, getting married, relocating to a foreign nation, and commencing grad school—these were big transitions within a short span of time in my mid-twenties, shaping a pivotal phase in my life.

I graduated as the financial crisis was unfolding in the US in 2008. Companies went on a hiring freeze, and we were contemplating moving back to India. Had it not been for a phone call I received the day I graduated offering me a job in fraud risk management at American Express, our lives would have unfolded differently.

Because of this job, I was able to travel to India for my brother's wedding and see my family for the first time in two years, pay back my student debt, and save enough for a down payment to buy our first home—a dream come true as an immigrant. Life was back on track after I had uprooted myself from India four years earlier, with new friendships and networks we'd formed in America. We were ready to become parents, although the child we hoped for didn't come along for years.

When I faced challenges in conceiving, I felt desperate, ashamed, inadequate, and lonely at the possibility of never having my own biological child. Adopting a child while on a visa wasn't straightforward. Eventually, we got our green cards and visited India for the second time in six years. This time, we squeezed in a trip to Tirupati (home to a holy shrine for Hindus) in Andhra Pradesh, long overdue to honor our family tradition. Lo and behold, I was pregnant a month later when we were back in the US. Whether it was the travel with my in-laws to the shrine for God Almighty's blessing or a glass of scotch that worked its magic, it remains a mystery to date!

The next year was joyful and tumultuous, with our parents visiting the US from India to be with our newborn, Aryan Kabir Gupta, so we could continue with our jobs. As if my journey to get pregnant, become a mom, and raise a boy with a full-time job wasn't hard enough, the untimely death of one of my immediate family members in an accident left us completely devastated. My parents had to rush back to India, and Aryan transitioned to a Montessori overnight. Before Aryan turned one, Arnab started his executive MBA at Thunderbird alongside his full-time job. What I had learned from my grandparents was that it takes a village (literally) to raise a family, and I needed to create my own village, no matter where I was.

Living in a foreign land, working, and traveling with a toddler wouldn't have been feasible had it not been for the community we had built, including dear friends like the Basus. We met the Basus a few years prior at a Dandiya event (a traditional dance from Gujarat) during Navratri, a Hindu festival celebrating victory for goddess Durga over demons, in Phoenix. They had just moved from India, and we slowly built a relationship over the years. The Basus became our chosen family. When I traveled to the UK for a work trip, they were the ones I trusted to pick up Aryan from his Montessori school on days Arnab needed assistance. Shaily's mom was also in town then, and both of them would open their kitchen and heart to him. More than ever, I felt blessed to have a support system in place for us to live life far away from our home and loved ones.

As part of Arnab's coursework, he had the option to go to Beijing and Shanghai for an industry project. By then, I had already been at American Express for six years, completed a new stint in marketing analytics for small businesses, intentionally secured growth opportunities, and traveled to Canada and the UK for business trips. Right after being back from maternity leave, I was on my third stint in a new functional area leading product development. My new boss was amazing, and I had known him since I joined the company. He was the first person who taught me the technical aspects of a magnetic stripe in a credit card. But he wasn't just great at work; he also taught me the simple joys of camping with our families in the middle of nowhere, a quintessentially American thing.

However, as much as I loved my new job, I wasn't going to let it, or my toddler, be a reason for missing out on this China adventure with Arnab. If my parents could travel throughout India on a bus with two small kids, feeding us and making beds for us on the floor of the moving bus in an era of no cell phones, bad roads, and no internet, traveling on a plane in the 21st century sounded like a piece of cake.

Being a global citizen at heart, I decided that Aryan and I would join Arnab on this trip, a week before Arnab's projects were scheduled to start. In essence, Arnab had a different travel itinerary than Aryan and I—I got to travel with my munchkin on my lap. Our flights were mostly uneventful, except for the one where Aryan threw up on one of the flights and then kept calling the person sitting next to me Baba (dad). Any man was Baba for Aryan!

Our friend KB was attending the same program at Thunderbird as Arnab, and he opted for the same foreign experience in China. We had traveled together with the Basus in Arizona years ago and couldn't wait for this next adventure together.

Despite our prior travel experiences, four adults and a toddler traveling in a country where none of us spoke Mandarin felt like a stretch. Growing up in India, all four of us spoke three or four different languages, but English was the common thread that connected us when we traveled, at least in bigger cities (courtesy of colonialism). But that wasn't the case in China. Thankfully, Shaily had the foresight to research and hire a local guide even before we landed in China. Our guide drove the five of us in her own car to all the places: Tiananmen Square, the Summer Palace, the Great Wall of China. We had other considerations to factor in: since YouTube and Google were blocked in China, we downloaded Youku, a Chinese version of YouTube, on our tablet to keep Aryan entertained. Living in democracies throughout my life, I had taken certain privileges for granted. Yet, here I was in a country where some of these things were not available.

We arrived in Beijing right around Chinese New Year. Our guide told us that people from faraway villages in China usually visit Tiananmen Square around that time. When we arrived at the Square, I noticed many villagers smiling at us. One group came forward and gestured that they wanted a picture with us, including Aryan. Our guide translated that the villagers were admiring "Aryan's big eyes." Arnab and I exchanged a look and laughed. Around these villagers, we felt a sense of simplicity that was very familiar to us as we had grown up in small towns. I wondered about the career prospects for my toddler with his big, bright eyes as he grew up. I said, "Imagine if Aryan learned Mandarin and became a singer or an artist. He could collectively communicate with over two billion people (in Bengali, English, Hindi, and Mandarin) and receive so much love, attention, and money. And we could simply relax!" We shared a good laugh.

Beijing is known for its air pollution, but the week prior to us arriving in Beijing, it had rained, so we didn't experience the usual high levels. We were pleasantly surprised to enjoy clear blue skies the whole time we were there. As our pedicab (tiny rickshaw) flew on the streets near Tiananmen Square, I felt a cold chill and mystery in the air thinking about the massacre that had taken place in the late 80s. I held Aryan's tiny body close in my arms. His head resting near my heart provided a sense of warmth and comfort.

We were staying at the Regent Hotel in Beijing, one of the most luxurious hotels I've stayed in. The hotel spa was open twenty-four hours. Why didn't more hotels offer spa services at night so tourists, moms, or parents could avail of them? When there was so much to explore during the day in such a limited time, I didn't have time to go to the spa. But because of the extended hours at this hotel, I got to treat myself. Arnab and I took turns, one of us watching Aryan while the other slipped out of the room to get a massage. Aryan barely slept for four hours straight at most each night, and I was sleep-deprived and jet-lagged with the fifteen-hour time difference. So, I must have conked out in my room after the heavenly massage for I have no recollection whatsoever.

Food in China ended up being a pleasant delight for me. Prior to this trip, I had always equated Chinese food with what I grew up eating from roadside Indian dhabas along the highways and what I used to relish on Camac Street in Kolkata, which included chilly chicken, egg noodles, and spicy chicken Manchurian. I got my first taste of authentic Chinese food at Thunderbird when a friend of mine invited us over for a home-cooked meal, all prepared tableside. I smiled to myself, thinking how different and delicious this food was from what I used to equate Chinese food with.

Our guide in Beijing was extremely knowledgeable, and we got to delight in lots of different meals. I don't recall the name of one of the restaurants she took us to, but hands down, it was one of the most delicious meals I've ever had in my life. The place seemed to know that Indian neighbors were visiting them, as they served us something very similar to paratha (a type of Indian bread). With our guide's help navigating the menu, we ordered cauliflower curry with pork and some dumplings. As I looked around, the people dining there smiled as we made eye contact. They looked very different from me. Yet, I felt welcomed and connected to their culture through this meal.

Without our guide, we made our way to the silk and pearl markets, infamous spots for bargain goods in Beijing. Having been raised in India, bargaining and negotiating for a good deal is familiar to me. I am happy to pay a premium for excellent quality, but I also have an eye for a good deal. At one of the shops we visited, a seller quoted us a price of 5,000 yuan for some item, and Shaily and I countered with a very bold counter-offer of ten yuan. KB and Arnab looked at us, embarrassed. But, to their surprise, the seller dropped the price to 1,000 yuan, and we upped our offer to twenty yuan. We ended up buying that item for fifty-eight yuan; I can't remember exactly how much now; that wasn't the point. These men couldn't believe what they saw us doing, and their embarrassment soon turned to sheer admiration. Totally worth the risk! At another shop, my bargaining powers didn't work as well. I offended the shopkeeper by offering too low of a price for a travel bag I wanted, and he refused to sell it to me, feeling lowballed. I felt guilty, so I went back to the shop and ended up buying it at a slightly higher price. Here's to conducting business, negotiating, and attempting to repair relationships through creative ways of communicating, all without knowing the language.

As our time in Beijing came to an end, we said goodbye to our guide, and we hired a taxi to take us to the train station to buy tickets for the bullet train to Shanghai the next day. As I was waiting near the ticket counter, an old woman started talking to me. The language barrier felt real; I could tell she was kind. For the life of me, I could not understand what she was trying to ask me. She gestured to me to wait, and as she walked away, I simply kept staring at her in bewilderment. Before I knew it, she pointed to the pictures of a boy and a girl hanging in a shop nearby, then turned to point at Aryan, raising her hand in the air for me to answer. Oh, she was asking me whether Aryan was a boy or a girl! I pointed to the picture of the boy, and she smiled, blessed us, and disappeared into the crowd.

Humans have been communicating through signs, sounds, touch, emotions, and other non-verbal cues without perfect words or language since time immemorial. Although I didn't speak the language, I felt the love around the villagers at Tiananmen Square, the warmth in that restaurant full of people, and the connection with this woman going the extra mile to talk to me through pictures. I loved my time in Beijing and was a bit sad that it was time to leave, and yet excited to see what Shanghai had in store for us.

When we took the bullet train from Beijing to Shanghai, the train traveled over 1,300 kilometers (800+ miles) in about four and a half hours, an engineering marvel indeed. I was amazed as it used to take me nearly twenty-four hours to cover a similar distance from Ranchi to Delhi via train while in college! The landscape between the two megalopolises included empty lands, ghost towns, and tall buildings. When we arrived in Shanghai, it was raining, and I don't think it ever stopped raining for the three days we were there. We bought umbrellas to survive the weather.

A four-hour-long sumptuous meal at South Beauty, the most popular Szechuan restaurant in Shanghai, was the highlight of our time there. When our cab dropped us near the restaurant, we couldn't find its entrance, but luckily, a stranger walked around the garden and showed us the way in. The building was a glass-house-like dome structure surrounded by gardens. The server took our drink order; we asked for water, beer, and wine—we only got water and beer. As we started our meal, KB needed a fork and asked for one, but they didn't understand. He literally had to walk over to show them a fork and knife in a nearby drawer. We inquired about the wine we had ordered (by now, we were pros at figuring out how to communicate without knowing the language) and learned an important cultural lesson that day: we could only choose one drink at a time, at least that's the lesson we took away. Besides, we had ordered way too much food. So, the wine had to wait until we finished our meal.

We visited the tallest building, Shanghai Tower. The observation deck is 159 meters high. I went to an area in the tower with a see-through glass floor that you can step out on. I summoned the courage to walk on the glass to see below, and Arnab stood far away, cringing as I set my foot in the center. I felt a bit dizzy looking down but chose to enjoy the view at eye level. Since I had faced my fears, we went to a famous Chinese restaurant called Din Tai Fung to celebrate. I love dumplings and ordered seven dishes on the menu! I was still breastfeeding and clearly eating for two humans, plus I felt I deserved this feast after my daring adventure at the Shanghai Tower and acknowledging how lucky I was to have this grand meal.

Of all the places I have visited in my life, China remains the most memorable. Moving past the assumptions I had made about her before the trip, I witnessed amazing infrastructure development. Immigration checks in Beijing and Shanghai felt like a breeze with designated counters for parents traveling with kids. There were security cameras all along the corridors with facial recognition and AI, and personally, I felt they were using technology to make travel easier. Despite the amazing infrastructure that we often take for granted in the US, I was impressed with the investments China had made into infrastructure and transportation to connect people across the vast country. I came back home to Phoenix a different person than the one who had boarded the plane to Beijing, with a lot more admiration for this ancient civilization and appreciation for my parents who, despite their humble beginnings, made it a priority to travel with me from a young age each year in an era when it wasn't as easy to travel.

Fast forward three years, my life came to a crossroads. Adaptability, resourcefulness, creativity, and problem-solving skills gained through my many adventures also enabled me to rise in my corporate career, and yet, I was completely burnt out. So, I invested energy in the inner work through therapy, coaching, energy healing, breathwork, and many other lifestyle changes, including meditation and exercise; all worthwhile investments to claim all of myself back—the free-spirited child who was resilient, thrived on learning new perspectives, and yearned for greater ease, connection, and trust in life. This led me to launch my business for transformation and healing in this world, creating trust and connection through consulting, coaching, public speaking, and retreats that allow me to travel and explore.

As this book goes to print, Aryan is turning ten. The trips we've taken together in the last decade have been a source of joy for us, and I know we're passing down our wanderlust to him, just like my parents did for me all those years ago.

Life is full of unknowns. I didn't know that we would live to see a pandemic where travel ceased, and where I would long to be near our loved ones. I didn't know that I wouldn't get to see my paternal grandmother, Annapurna Gupta, before she passed away. Or that after sixteen years in Phoenix, we would move to Austin to start our lives yet again in a new place.

Through all of these unknowns, I'm reminded that life is a gift, and the next moment is not guaranteed. The places I have visited, the people I've met, and the experiences I've encountered in my life have shaped me. Dad once said, "Traveling opens your mind. New places bring new energy. You should travel. To know this earth. To know how big this earth is. You are never too young or too old to travel." I experienced that firsthand by witnessing the vastness of this earth, from the seas to the majestic Wall of China.

KALPASHREE GUPTA

Kalpashree Gupta is a public speaker, writer, coach, and consultant. As the CEO of Knekxt Group, she helps clients build trust and create awareness for leaders who have used their achievements to deflect from dealing with trauma. She experienced childhood sexual abuse, and her vision for this world is to transform and heal so billions of people can reclaim their personal power, use their voice, and create a kinder world.

Kalpa has twenty years of experience in leadership and executive roles within Fortune 500 companies in the financial services and healthcare industries. Born in a mining town in India, she now lives in Austin with her husband, Arnab, and their nine-year-old son, Aryan.

Website: knekxt.com/

LinkedIn: www.linkedin.com/in/kalpashreegupta/

TikTok: https://www.tiktok.com/@knekxt.com

CHILDREN'S EMERGENCY SHELTER

All proceeds from this multi-author book are donated to Central Texas Table of Grace.

Central Texas Table of Grace is a 501(c)(3) non-profit organization that exists to provide emergency shelter services to the foster children and administers Grace365 Supervised Independent Living program for young adults aging out of foster care. Their support contributes to an improved quality of life for youth and their families. The organization's projects, implemented by an experienced staff, emphasize creating a caring climate for youth. Supporting the development of self-confidence, healthful living, and good judgment, Central Texas Table of Grace provides our children with a thorough foundation for success.

Follow Central Texas Table of Grace on social media to find out more.

https://www.facebook.com/centraltexastableofgrace

https://www.instagram.com/ctxtableofgrace/

https://www.linkedin.com/company/central-texas-table-of-grace/

https://twitter.com/CTXTableOfGrace

https://www.tiktok.com/@ctxtableofgrace

ABOUT SULIT PRESS

S ulit Press is a boutique publishing house that provides high-touch support to thought leaders, industry shakers, and changemakers writing impactful nonfiction books. Whether you're interested in publishing your **personal memoir** or industry-specific **solo books,** or joining high-vibe, collaborative **multi-author books**, we'll help you transition from *aspiring* author to *published* author!

Founder and CEO Michelle Savage is an international best-selling author, editor, and author mentor. From her experience of walking authors through the publishing process with other publishing houses, Michelle discovered a gaping hole in the market—finding publishers who care enough about their authors to provide a cohesive publishing process and deliver on their promises. Sulit Press was born from Michelle's desire to create a boutique publishing space that offers personalized support through every step and invests deeply in the success of every single author.

www.ingramcontent.com/pod-product-compliance
Lightning Source LLC
Chambersburg PA
CBHW030253130626
46549CB00002B/505